Outrageous Optimism

Wisdom for the Entrepreneurial Journey

Jack Roseman
&
Steve Czetli

First Edition
Corbett Publishing * Pittsburgh * PA

www.rosemaninstitute.com

Outrageous Optimism
Wisdom for the Entrepreneurial Journey

Jack Roseman & Steve Czetli

Published by:
Corbett Publishing
Pittsburgh, PA

ISBN: 0-9745135-1-2

Table of Contents

Dedication..v
Acknowledgments...vii
Foreward..ix
Introduction..xi
- 1: What it Takes...1
- 2: Mission or Money?..................................5
- 3: Dreamers & Doers...................................9
- 4: Bitten by the Bug..................................13
- 5: Life Lessons...17
- 6: How Big?...21
- 7: How Big II..25
- 8: Unconventional Capital..........................29
- 9: Starting with Nothing.............................31
- 10: Control...35
- 11: Partners & Power.................................39
- 12: Timing...43
- 13: Follow-up vs Pestering.........................47
- 14: Titles..51
- 15: Mission..55
- 16: Strategic Planning...............................59
- 17: Ugly Babies..63
- 18: Letting Go..67
- 19: Respect...71
- 20: Price Point...75
- 21: Sales Forecasts...................................79
- 22: David vs Goliath..................................83
- 23: Tearjerker..87
- 24: Problem Board Members........................91
- 25: Ideal Board Members............................95
- 26: Ideal CEOs...97
- 27: Recognition.......................................101

Table of Contents (con't)

- 28: Decision-Making......................................105
- 29: Sweet Spot...107
- 30: Loyalty...111
- 31: Attitude..115
- 32: Worrier or Warrior....................................119
- 33: Service...123
- 34: Paradigms...127
- 35: Santa Claus Syndrome..................................131
- 36: Motivation..135
- 37: Self-worth..139
- 38: Making Acquisitions Work..............................143
- 39: A Higher Authority....................................145
- 40: Outrageous Optimism...................................147
- 41: Wake-Up Call..151

Roseman

Dedication

This book is dedicated to my wife, Judy, who for forty-four years has endured being the spouse of an entrepreneur.

She understood that in order for me to be true to myself, I had no choice, none; but to take the journey of an entrepreneur.

During the journey, she was never phased by the turns of a new venture. She was my counsel, advisor, confidant and a steadfast rock when I needed one.

Jack Roseman

To my wife Kathy, a gift to all who know her.

Steve Czetli

Acknowledgments

First and foremost I would like to thank Steve Czetli, for his role in the creation of these essays. He has a unique talent for drawing out stories long-forgotten and for helping me make points I have taken for granted for so long that I sometimes failed to see their usefulness for a new generation of entrepreneurs. Steve has been able to corral my thoughts and capture my unique way of saying things so that the voice is as authentic as the ideas.

I am also grateful to Saras Saraswarthy, a former Ph.D. student at Carnegie Mellon University, who spent countless hours with me discussing, joking and debating entrepreneurial and ethical issues. Much of her is contained in this one quote from some 15 years ago: "Jack, each book I read opens another door to heaven." I appreciate her continued friendship. Of course, I have also learned from all of my students and would be remiss not to credit them with shaping any wisdom that the reader finds in this book. The same should be said for associates, clients, and others who provided much of the material that makes the experiences retold in this book relevant and significant.

Thanks, too, to all the readers who have found these articles useful and were kind enough to tell me so. All these people truly encouraged me to continue.

A special thanks to Suzanne Caplan, a prolific author of business books and savvy entrepreneur who guided me through the book publishing maze that faces any writer bold enough to bundle up his own words and peddle them to the general public. I am also grateful to my daughter Shari Roseman, and Susan Farrington for proofreading the manuscript.

Jack Roseman

Foreward

This book is a collection of vignettes from the life of Jack Roseman. Jack's a real entrepreneur who built real businesses, and in the process constructed a life full of values, passions, and friendships. Raised in a Massachusetts ghetto by a family deeply affected by the holocaust (many of his family members perished in the holocaust, including a brother and most of his extended family) Jack worked his way through two degrees in mathematics, held positions at MIT and GE and then built several technology companies, starting at a time when you would walk into a computer that was larger than most apartments today.

This book is NOT an instructional manual on how to accumulate millions of dollars. It is an invitation to take a journey into entrepreneurship as a way of life. And it is not much use refusing the invitation. When confronted with a "No," Jack will likely tilt his head to one side, look you straight in the eye and say, "What an interesting way to start a relationship."

Despite his passion for work, to travel with Jack is not a hurried flight of fancy hobnobbing with those who dabble in oil futures and dot-com bubbles. It is more like a civilized train trip with time to pause and reflect over cups of coffee and start meaningful conversations with strangers.

Whether you are already on your entrepreneurial journey, simply contemplating the trip or wanting to come along merely for the view, consider this book your travel companion. As the train leaves the station, Jack will point out to you some precautions you need to take, describe the curious flora and fauna you might encounter and suggest how to deal with unruly passengers. He will share with you his experiences about hiring and motivating people, choosing partners, buying and selling a business, negotiating deals and obtaining financing. He will share with you how to deal with setbacks and failure – even his own which struck at 42. He will talk to you candidly about the most important aspects of starting and running your own business while at the same time building a worthwhile life.

Throughout this journey, as you get to know your travel companion better, you will find that besides the integrity, imagination, humor, intelligence and attention to detail that have served him so well in business, at the foundation of Jack's character lies a fundamental optimism that in the final analysis may be the defining quality of all successful entrepreneurs. As you will see from many of these stories, it often seems unwarranted, which is why in Jack's case he has named his book "Outrageous Optimism." It is optimism so profound that it holds up in the face of the inevitable ups and downs of business, through the deception of trusted partners, disappointments by dear friends and the other blows that await each of us as we set out on the journey of life, what might be called the extreme journey of entrepreneurship.

If you are worrying about failure on either journey, by the time you are done with this book, Jack will make it very difficult for you not to bet on yourself. To put it in his own words, "If an elephant knew its own strength, would we be able to hold it in place with a little stump and a pitiful piece of rope?"

If you are ready to snap the rope and confront the elephant within yourself, come spend an easy hour or two listening to the real stories of a real entrepreneur. "All aboard!"

Saras D. Sarasvathy, Ph.D.

Roseman

Introduction

I invite you to take a journey with me, one intended to lead you down the path to success. This is a journey that has its ups and downs, includes ecstasies as well as agonies. Along the way, we will explore the question of how to define success; handling new found wealth, luxurious houses & cars, a satisfying family life and good friends, peace of mind or the amount of good work done for society. When you are finished, I hope you will have a better perspective on each.

When Steve Czetli began interviewing me for a monthly column called "Entrepreneur's Corner" that first appeared in early 1997 in T.E.Q. Magazine, the monthly publication of The Pittsburgh Technology Council, and later, for a monthly column that appeared in the "Pittsburgh Post-Gazette," I had no idea that we would end up writing so many of them. What surprised me even more was the warmth and depth of responses I have received from readers.

Eventually, people began asking me to put these essays together in one place. And when we took on the task of stitching them together, I became more convinced that the principles that guided my life may very well add value to yours.

You have chosen a book about success. While you will find tips and techniques that should enhance your wealth, this is not the typical "how to" book about growing sales and increasing profits. Instead, it is about enriching your business life as well as the world around you.

If you use some of my ideas, that's fine. It would even be better if you build on these ideas and refine them to make them work for you. Incorporate them into your work and your life.

Whether you are an entrepreneur who wants to become more skilled in building your business, an executive who wants to live more entrepreneurially, or even someone who is curious about entrepreneurship and whether it is right for you, this book has something to offer.

One of the most satisfying aspects of teaching has been the opportunity to meet with people face to face. I really enjoy the individual experience that is the bend of your head, the tone of your voice, the warmth of your handshake. I wish I could sit across the table from each and everyone of you and we could discuss your entrepreneurial questions over a cup of coffee. But of course that is impractical. So I am counting on you to make the most of our encounter through the book in your hands.

I learned my most profound lessons about life at a time when I almost lost mine. Thirty years ago, I had a massive heart attack and wasn't expected to live through the night. For me, that was a new beginning and since then I have continued to be productive, starting my third company, becoming a chaired professor at Carnegie Mellon University, the resident mentor at a business incubator and ultimately, starting my own consulting group, The Roseman Institute, a subsidiary of a prestigious law firm, Buchanan Ingersoll, P.C. I spend much of my time consulting with other company founders and I work now, as I always have, with passion.

That passion, once the driving force of a workaholic, is now directed toward many more areas of my life: family, friends, students, community and my own well-being. Today entrepreneurship may be at the center of my life, but these many other activities help to keep it in balance.

I genuinely welcome your thoughts and comments. Please feel free to contact me at: rosemanj@rosemaninstitute.com

Jack Roseman

"There are some things which cannot be learned quickly, and time, which is all we have, must be paid heavily for their acquiring. They are the very simplest things, and because it takes a man's life to know them, the little that each man gets from life is very costly and the only heritage he has to leave."

—Ernest Hemingway

Outrageous Optimism

Wisdom for the Entrepreneurial Journey

1. What It Takes

The question I am most often asked is: What does it take to be a successful entrepreneur?

The answer is always somewhat unsatisfying. You can read books on it. You can take college courses in it. You can spend a lifetime learning the answer by trial and error. You can find a mentor — somebody who has done it before. They will all provide a piece of the puzzle, but I also can name people who have taken every one of these approaches and failed to become successful entrepreneurs.

Entrepreneurship isn't so easy. If it was, we'd all be entrepreneurs. Why not? Why wouldn't we want to be our own boss, make a million bucks and have people do what we tell them? Sound good? It does to a lot of people who decide every day that they are going to be entrepreneurs. Some fail in one year, some fail in two years, and some fail in five years. Some fail in the sense that they have to sell out within a few years. Many more have dreams about becoming entrepreneurs but never take the first step. But a handful do. And some succeed. Occasionally beyond their wildest expectations.

So what is an entrepreneur? It is a word that gets thrown around a lot today, but what really qualifies someone as an entrepreneur? A one-store retailer? A woodworker? A franchisee? Anyone who has become financially independent from an enterprise, no matter how modest or lucky?

If we are looking for the enduring principles, universal skill sets and personal characteristics that lead to success as an entrepreneur, it is best to set a high standard. That way we are less likely to be confused by those who got lucky, those who didn't play by the rules or those who succeeded in spite of themselves.

So when I look for what it takes to be a successful entrepreneur, I ask, what does it take to build a Medrad or a Respironics? Neither of those companies started out gangbusters. For each, it was a slow process, but Steve Heilman at Medrad and Gerry McGinnis at Respironics demonstrated uncommon perseverance, and today Medrad and Respironics are both global, publicly traded companies. So, I think it's safe to say perseverance is a good quality to have if you want to build a world-class company from scratch.

Other characteristics that meet the standard include outstanding communication skills. You have to be able to sell your vision to customers, investors and employees, and you have to understand human nature. That means you have to understand yourself. If you understand yourself, you will be able to trust yourself — and that's a big part of being a successful entrepreneur. You need to be able to trust your instincts.

But not to the exclusion of what the smart people around you are saying. You absolutely must have an open ear to what the world is telling you. And usually that's a whisper compared with what you want to hear.

Partners you trust can be a big help in this. These days you absolutely need partners and advisers who can help you see the big picture, and who can shore up areas where you don't have enough specialized knowledge or experience to make good decisions. Then you have to be flexible and open-minded enough to listen to them.

This is a big one. You have to know the difference between an idea and an opportunity. Many people go into business when it is not a business. It may be a good idea, but not a good business. What makes the difference is whether people will buy your product, and whether they will buy from *you*. Is it a "must buy" or a "like to buy" product or service? If they are willing to buy something already on the market for $10 and I've got something that's twice as good for $5, then I know they'll buy.

But that's not the only analysis. You have to ask whom you are going to come up against as competitors. What is your competitive advantage? What is your point of differentiation? Unless you truly understand why people will buy and why people will buy from *you,* you haven't determined whether this is a good business or just an interesting idea. You would be surprised how hard it is for some entrepreneurs to separate their love for their idea from a realistic judgment about whether it's a sustainable business.

Successful entrepreneurs possess a rare combination of characteristics that we don't often see in people. So when people ask me what it takes to be a successful entrepreneur, I am reminded of just how challenging it is. The question that occurs to me is: Why are there any successful entrepreneurs?

2. Mission or Money?

From the outside it probably seems like entrepreneurs are only chasing money and that they go into business for the sole purpose of accumulating great sums of the stuff. I'm sure there are some who are drawn to entrepreneurship for the money, but I can tell you that among the entrepreneurs I have mentored and certainly in my own experience, money has been a by-product. Or I should say, when the venture was successful it was a by-product.

The truth is most entrepreneurs I know aren't chasing money as much as they are pursuing a vision. Of course, some of those visions are more grandiose than others, and that's fine. Some people are excited by what Bill Gates did, but others are quite content owning a two-person consulting company. You see, for a lot of entrepreneurs, their dream may simply be to wake up in the morning and do something they love. To be able to make a reasonable living at what you love isn't a bad way to live. That's at one end of the spectrum.

At the other end is a more complex organization that brings together a lot of people with different talents and dreams of their own. You pick them and organize them to effectively achieve your dream. If you're smart, you won't hire anybody who doesn't buy into your dream. You need a common vision nowadays to make an organization function competitively. Especially when you are starting out, you need every competitive edge you can get.

I have always felt strongly about employees believing in my dream. At Actronics, my last startup, I required that all early employees take a pay cut to work for me. I figured that was one way to know for sure that they believed in my vision.

Now if the dream comes true, there's plenty of money for

everybody, but it's a mistake to work solely for the money. Work for the dream. You'll get more out of people if you excite their imagination than if you say, "I'm going to give you a bonus." My own excitement came from pioneering in new technology fields by creating a product or service that had not existed before, or applying technology in a new way. If I did not have a passion for the value we were bringing to the marketplace, I rejected the idea. I firmly believe success requires that the entrepreneur be excited about what he or she is doing. If there is no excitement, there is no spark to ignite the fire.

I once ran into a young man on the Carnegie Mellon University campus just as he was giving out this great sigh. It was the kind of sigh that signaled he was not too happy with his life at the moment and I said to him, "You're too young to sigh like that." He said, "I've got two more days, then I can live." Since this was a Thursday, I surmised he was looking forward to the weekend. My concern was that this young man will always be saying, "Two more days and I can live."

How many days of his life will he really live? I'm afraid he will develop the mindset of always putting hurdles between himself and what it is that he truly enjoys doing. How many people live for the weekend, just like this young man?

Of course there are many factors that must be taken into account when you are deciding whether to make a commitment to a new business. You have to consider barriers to entry, capitalization, timing and competitive advantage among others, but there are plenty of people and books to advise you on those subjects. What I want to get across is that your own personal excitement about the project should be your first criteria. You have got to enjoy coming to work everyday, because you will be spending a lot of your life there.

Do something that excites you. Maybe it won't succeed, but at least in the meantime you've enjoyed the huge part of your life that it ate up. At least if you love what you are doing, you have spent each day in eager anticipation of the next. That to me is what life is all about.

3. Dreamers & Doers

Do you really want to be an entrepreneur? Many of the people who come to me with an idea for a business really don't. They say they do, but in truth lack the fire in their belly to step over the threshold. They are held back by an often invisible barrier of excuses and rationalizations. Instead of a fire in their bellies, they have butterflies.

Think of this range of entrepreneurs as a spectrum. At one end are people who never even consider going into business for themselves. They want to work for a bank, a PPG, Alcoa or Mellon. Then there are a bunch of other people who fantasize — *wouldn't it be nice to have my own company?* I have talked to one friend no fewer than a dozen times about starting a company. The last time I told him to forget it and get a good job. If he was going to start a company, he would have done it years ago. It eventually became clear to me that he was in love with the fantasy of starting his own company, not actually doing it.

One of my former students came to me recently and said he wasn't sure if it was the right time for him to start a company, so he thought he might go back to school and get an MBA. That way, he said, he'd be a better entrepreneur. But what you learn about actually starting a company from rolling up your sleeves and doing it, you are never going to learn in an MBA program.

This young man's mother had died of cancer, and later his father passed away. He was 31, single and had no children.

So I said to him, "When are you going to be in a better position to start a company? You're telling me you want to go to school for three years — get some more experience and by the time you're done, it will be four or five years later, and by that time you might be married and have children. How will you be in a better position to start a company? You're kidding yourself. If you are going to start a company, there is no more opportune time than now."

Those people are in the middle of the spectrum.

On the other end are people like me who don't have a choice. People for whom that burning desire to be on their own, to do their own thing, is so strong that risk be damned, we are going to do it and do it now!

Are we adrenaline junkies?

I admit I like the excitement. That's true. There have been studies that found a disproportionate number of entrepreneurs had attention deficit disorder (ADD). They are easily bored. They are not the best students and they make lousy employees. I've never been diagnosed with ADD, but in a lot of respects, that's me.

I also have a need to be in charge of my destiny. If I am successful, I want to know that I did it.

But there is more. I also want the bonding experience that occurs when you do it with people you like and respect. The people I went into business with became like brothers to me. They were comrades. I like the feeling of being part of a small group of people against the world. I used to see my partners and the key people in the company a lot more than I ever saw my wife. In fact, my business partners and I lived with each other day and night. Whatever it took we were all in the same boat.

I told you that money was never a driving issue with me, and that's true. But I will also tell you that I have an ego and that has been part of what's driving the train.

From my office window, I can plainly see a sign on a building that says "FreeMarkets." Do I think the CEO, Glen Meakem, had only the welfare of his company in mind when he negotiated to put that sign up there? I don't think so. I think that's also his ego speaking, but that's common among entrepreneurs. I'm going to build something and when I'm finished, it's part of me.

As an entrepreneur, you get a rush of positive feeling when you bring in a big order or win a contract over an arch-rival; think of a niche that Dell, Intel or Microsoft overlooked. Those are all high moments.

So people start companies for many different reasons, with a host of motivations. But at the core, I believe every true entrepreneur is doing what they have to do. If they don't have to do it, they don't. Instead they fantasize about it and make excuses why they can't do it just then.

4. Bitten by the Bug

Early in my career, I was married and living in the Washington D.C. area where part of my job was to supervise more than 100 computer scientists at a national computer services firm. A prime responsibility was to quote work and see that it got done on time with a reasonable profit margin.

I operated on the belief that professionals worked best when allowed to set their own schedules. So as long as they delivered, the people in my division operated on a version of flextime. I would explain the job and ask when the customer could expect it. Usually my associates would say something like, "Oh, Jack, no big deal. I can get that out in two months."

The reason I was very good at estimating costs was that I always added an optimism factor before pricing the job. These were bright, responsible people so, typically, when my scientists and engineers found themselves falling behind, they would ratchet up their efforts, often working day and night. That effort, combined with my optimism factor, resulted in met deadlines and the most profitable division in the company. It also kept my crew happy and productive.

My boss, however, had a different philosophy of management. It bothered him that on the occasions when he would show up in my division at 9 a.m., half or more of the staff was absent.

"Hey Jack," he said one day. "You're not running a tight ship here."

"But we're the most profitable division," I replied. "No one is close to our profitability."

"Yes," he replied, "but can you imagine how much *more* money you would make if you were on their backs?"

This was not the first disagreement we had. Once this man had stopped by to tell me that he wanted ten milestones for all projects.

"That doesn't make sense," I explained to him. "What we do, for instance, is if it's a $5,000 contract, it might only have one milestone and if it's a million dollar contract, we might have twenty milestones."

"No," he replied, "All projects from now on will have ten milestones."

"Why ten?" I asked. "Why not nine?"

Rolling his eyes skyward as if unable to comprehend my denseness, he measured his words. "Jack, didn't I tell you I thought of ten, not nine?"

I cannot take working for this guy, I thought to myself. I *might as well be arguing with my young children.*

Of course, something parallel had occurred to him. The next time we talked it was to introduce me to my replacement. I was demoted and shuttled from my oversized office – one of the greatest pleasures of my life – to a good-sized closet down the hall. I went home that day convinced I would just have to resign.

"Why do you have to resign?" asked Judy, my wife.

"You don't understand," I explained, "People work for me, I don't work for them. In this reorganization I am now low – below low."

"Jack," she said, "If you think these people respected and worked so well for you because you were a boss, then you should leave tomorrow. If you think they respected you for who you are, then you have no reason to leave. You can't leave a job just because you don't feel appreciated. If you are going to be in the business world, you had better learn how to take some setbacks."

I let this simmer overnight and by morning realized she was right. Faced with my first professional setback, I was not going to run away. But I was still angry.

"Okay," I said, "I am going to stay, and I'm going to stay until I get a huge promotion. The day I get that promotion is my last day."

In the meantime I decided to lay the groundwork for my own computer services company.

To make my demotion tolerable day to day, I tried to bury myself in work. Each morning I would arrive at my tiny office, transfer out enough books to permit me to squeeze in, and then concentrate on the day's tasks. This would work until a colleague walked by and attempted to cheer me up. Typically this consisted of some variation on, "Roseman. Boy, did you get screwed."

And then I would feel terrible again.

In the meantime, my replacement was making his own mark. He was a Dutchman who came with impressive academic credentials, an old world sense of discipline and a rigid view of how things were to be done. One day he walked into the office of our top scientist and pointed to an unframed painting hanging on the wall. "Eli," he said, "a picture worth hanging is worth framing. I give you one week to get it framed or take it down."

It was not long before Eli and the other top people found friendlier environments in which to write their code. Customers followed them and soon the company had fallen on hard times. My replacement and the executive who had demoted me were fired and I was summoned to the front office where a vice president offered me a position that would have put me in charge of all the company's offices nationwide. It was a substantial promotion.

The next day my resignation went in, because as luck would have it, I had just found someone willing to bankroll my own software company without requiring a controlling interest or terms that effectively put them in charge. And control had become very important to me. In fact, the whole experience was very important to me. What I had learned – in addition to the value of perseverance and believing in myself – was that more than anything, I wanted to run my own show.

5. Life Lessons

When you are young and trying to logically decide whether to become an entrepreneur or not, it's not uncommon to think of entrepreneurship as an isolated part of your life. You might think about the skills you need or the specific knowledge you need. What I don't think enough people consider is that entrepreneurial endeavors provide great training for life.

I genuinely believe that entrepreneurial training comes down to a lot of lessons in how to live. The whole series of experiences that you go through to start a company is about how you can become a more effective human being. They are about how you can be happy and successful in whatever you want to do.

At the beginning of the process there is an idea. Typically there is little else. You have no money, materials or people to help you. You just have an idea and you have to decide whether this will make a successful business or not. Isn't that how we start out in life?

To get those other things, you have to be able to communicate with other people logically and with passion. You have to think clearly. You have to position yourself and your idea as a winner.

You have to trot out your vision for what your company should be for angel investors, venture capitalists, prospective employees, and prospective customers and sometimes even suppliers. You have to explain your vision to spouses, friends, family, mentors and colleagues. You have to show how and why your business idea is better than the other ideas out there competing for their investment, talents, resources, time, attention, loyalty, friendship, trust and what not.

You have to communicate it so strongly, clearly and logically that those people will be willing to accept the risk of doing business with you instead of some other company.

And you have to plan. You have to be able to set up goals and measure your progress toward those goals. That means you are going to have to learn to make hard choices, set priorities and stick with them. It makes you peer into the future and decide what's important to you. It makes you project yourself onto your deathbed, from which you will look back at your life and make judgments so that you can say, "Well, I think I lived a pretty good life. I accomplished the things that I wanted to accomplish."

And it teaches you to be durable. The first lesson any entrepreneur must learn is things like the fact that "no" is just a little obstacle to a "yes." In life you have to toughen up, too, and not become easily dejected by rejection or setbacks.

Let me give you an example. Every semester when I was teaching at Carnegie Mellon, students called me about the entrepreneurship course I taught and would say, "I'd like to take your course, but I understand it's oversubscribed. May I take your course?" And I would say, "Well, haven't you answered your own question?" And they would say, "Thank you, Professor Roseman," and hang up. The truth is that there is always one more seat available. An entrepreneur understands that and doesn't give up. He or she doesn't accept "no."

You have to learn to not be easily discouraged. And when you fail, you have to learn how to get up, brush yourself off and go at it again even harder.

Entrepreneurship teaches you how to compete. That's important because as human beings we take a lot for granted. One thing we take for granted is that we have a right to exist. Our companies have to earn that right everyday. On day one, you don't have any business, and you have to take that business from somebody else. That's true everyday until you succeed, and then somebody will be trying to take your customers.

To compete effectively, you have to know yourself. That may not be immediately obvious, but you can't lead or motivate people until you understand yourself. Many people are born, live their whole lives fooling themselves, then die. An entrepreneur cannot afford to do that.

Entrepreneurs also cannot afford to look at their companies through any but the most objective, rational, accurate lens. It may be *your* baby, but you have to look at it very rationally, very objectively in terms of its strengths and weaknesses. You have to know where to put your resources and what partners you need to shore up deficiencies. How much better parents we are when we bring this kind of keen, honest appraisal to our own families.

I think entrepreneurship is a great way of life. But even if you don't end up with your own company, the lessons it teaches can improve whatever life you choose.

6. How Big?

My goal in life was to start a company that made it to the Big Board - a publicly traded business listed on the New York Stock Exchange. I didn't make it. The best I did was the American Exchange. But I have learned over the years that big isn't beautiful to everybody.

In my teaching career, I often come across students in entrepreneurship classes who have a unique talent and don't particularly want to work for someone else. It may be art, furniture-making or even computer programming. They want to know if they should pursue entrepreneurship.

I think entrepreneurship is doing something on your own at the level that you want to do it. If you want the headaches of building a large corporation and that's what turns you on, fine. That was the thing that turned me on. It wasn't the money; it was building something from scratch.

From my point of view, entrepreneurship is getting where *you* want to go. It's not where other people think you should go. If you want to be independent and not responsible for anyone else and you've got a business that can be successful on that basis – it's making as much money as you need and want – then you might be happier than Bill Gates.

The real question is what kind of company do *you* want to start? It was a question that came up with a talented furniture maker who took one of my entrepreneurship classes.

His satisfaction came from designing and making furniture. So when he wrote his business plan, it didn't provide for many employees. He could have other people perform manual labor, but when it came to things like assembling and finishing the furniture, he had to do it because that was what he enjoyed.

Well, his financial projections showed he would only make about $40,000 a year. A week or two after he submitted his business plan, he asked if he could talk to me.

He said, "What would you do?"

I said, "I would do the furniture." He was taken aback.

"But you're an entrepreneur," he said. "I am surprised that an entrepreneur would say to be satisfied with $40,000 a year." I explained my point. "Given the choice of making a million dollars and being unhappy or making $40,000 a year and feeling satisfied, doing something you enjoy, looking forward to going to work everyday, I would take the $40,000."

I recently had a young consultant come to me because he was considering going back to school for an MBA. He was successful — making $100,000 as a free-lance programmer/analyst. The MBA idea had been his father's, who was uneasy with the young man's job-to-job lifestyle.

"I love what I do," he said. "I've been at it 2 1/2 years, and I have no problem getting work. No one works for me. I love it."

"Why then are you even entertaining the notion of giving it up to get an MBA?" I asked.

"Maybe it will make me a better entrepreneur," he said.

I advised him to continue his consulting and take specific courses, but not to worry about the sheepskin. I do get a lot of entrepreneurs who say they want an MBA for peace of mind, so if they fail they can get a better job in the marketplace. This wasn't the case with this consultant. He was quite confident.

"Well then," I said. "Why do you have to go for an MBA? You're happy with what you're doing." Of course, most of the students at Carnegie Mellon wanted to be Bill Gates and make a whole lot of money. They wanted to have two or three houses and travel. They wanted to have the best car and the best this and the best that.

But these are smart people. Sooner or later they figure out that what they really want is happiness. If you ask their parents - who have the advantage of life experience – money is not what they want for them, it's happiness. And money won't buy you that happiness.

I think this fellow who is doing furniture is very happy; he loves what he can do with his own two hands.

And I think this consultant is very happy. In our conversation he said to me, " I just love being on my own, and if I can make $100,000 a year being my own man – why shouldn't I do that?" And there is no good reason at all why he shouldn't.

7. How Big II

I recently gave a lecture to a group of business owners, and the feedback I got surprised me. About half thought it was fine, but I found out through a friend of a friend that the feelings of the other half could be summed up as, "Very nice, Jack, but don't come back."

In all honesty, I thought I had done a great job, and the reaction buffaloed me. I asked the person who had shared this with me why the reaction hadn't been more positive. It seems I had left the impression that if you weren't going to be on the New York Stock Exchange, you were just a little kitten in a world of tigers.

Somehow I had made them feel that big is good and beautiful, and small is ugly and terrible. I didn't say that, and I don't feel that way, but obviously I communicated that message to this group by how I answered their questions and the way I spoke.

When I realized how I had come across, I completely understood their reaction. These were all successful entrepreneurs, and they rightfully felt pretty good about themselves. Then here I come pontificating about how important it is to be big and continue growing when they didn't want to grow anymore. They were happy.

A few days later I caught myself making the same mistake. A guy with a Western Pennsylvania business called me up to say he'd outgrown his bank and wanted me to recommend one. Actually, he'd been in business for 10 years and didn't need me to recommend a bank, but I took the opportunity to ask him why he wasn't growing his business outside the area. Why was he just in Western Pennsylvania? And he was very candid with me.

"Jack," he said, "I make $300,000 a year. That's more than I need. Why would I need more headaches?"

I find an awful lot of new entrepreneurs think that way reflexively. When I taught at Carnegie Mellon University and students would occasionally give me a business plan for a restaurant, it was almost always for one. I would ask, "Why not a chain?"

So why do I put so much emphasis on growth?

Because beginners think small. I don't expect everybody to think big, but I do like to make sure they have at least considered it, because a lot of people, entrepreneurs included, underestimate themselves and their capabilities. I think it's fine to say, "Get out of here, I'm satisfied with $300,000 a year, I've got enough headaches." I just wanted to make sure he had entertained the issue of being bigger.

And that's where people misunderstand what I'm saying. When you say you want one store, two stores, three stores, and I ask you to consider 100 stores, if you answer, "No, I don't," that's fine. What I'm afraid of is that most people never get to the point where they even ask that question. They are intimidated by size. One store is their horizon, and I think people should always push their horizon.

There is a practical side, too. If you are not a leader in your field, you will eventually die. I believe that. In some area you have to be the biggest, the best or both. If you don't keep an eye on what's going on around you, you will die. If you don't look at where your market is going, you can be a leader today and a goner tomorrow. You always have to have an eye to the future if you want to stick around.

Think about the fact that right here in Pittsburgh there had to be somebody making a good living in buggy whips who in the 1800s was thinking, "I'm going to be around forever; look how many buggy whips I'm selling." So you have to stay alert, and growing keeps you sharp.

I have to admit that some of it is purely personal. I grew up in poverty, and the challenge for me has always been, "How far can you go from nothing?" How do you escape the black hole of poverty and become a meteor? That desire had absolutely nothing to do with money. It was how big can you build something. I had in mind going public with every company I ever started. That was my measure of success.

There is an aspect of ego to it, too. If Bill Gates can build a Microsoft, why can't I? If somebody locally like Glen Meakem can build FreeMarkets, why can't I? Don't tell me they're smarter (although that may very well be true). Don't tell me they work harder because I don't buy it.

But here's the challenge with your ego: Harness it. Keep it going after the doughnut, not the hole in the doughnut. Don't try to win every battle; win the war. I see a lot of managers, supervisors and even CEOs who feel they have to win every argument. In the process they alienate the people whose support they need to make the company succeed.

Not everybody wants to be the biggest. That's not what is going to make them happy and they know it. In fact, one of my students in the entrepreneurial management program at Carnegie Mellon University some years ago had grown his business until he was at the top of its field, but in the process he had lost the spark that made going to work every day fun. He had taken my course in the hope of rekindling his enthusiasm. So every week I would ask him if he was having fun yet. The first several weeks the answer was "no." Then one night he came in, and I could just see that something dramatic had happened to him. "You're a different guy," I said to him. "You look like you're enjoying yourself." And indeed he was.

The difference? He had stepped down as CEO — turned it all over to somebody else — and returned to working with his hands, which was what he enjoyed in the first place.

8. Unconventional Capital

Most entrepreneurs without their own fortune or an independently wealthy family are very likely to see their business plan go begging for capital. That can be frustrating, especially when you're sure you've got the next Amazon.com.

If you're in that camp and a reasonable number of seasoned investors have given you a hearing but no money, you have to consider the fact that maybe they're telling you something that will save you a lot of time and money. I know that's hard to hear, but you owe it to yourself to consider it.

It may also be that you have the makings of a nice six-figure operation doing something you love and being your own boss - but investors don't see enough reward in it to take the risk of tying up their money. In that case, you could have a perfectly satisfactory basis for a business. Or maybe you've had offers of capital, but you don't want to dilute your ownership.

In either situation, here's a technique that has worked for me and for many of the entrepreneurs I have mentored. It puts your idea to a real-world test and keeps all the equity in your hands.

Get your capital from customers. Go to prospects and get them excited about the benefits of your product, that it will save them $30,000 a year or whatever, and when it hits the market it will sell for $60,000.

"But," you say, "we're currently raising capital and have a special arrangement for customers who pre-buy." You offer a deep discount of 50 percent, free maintenance, and say you will design it with features to ensure it specifically meets the needs of that prospect's particular operation.

Show her the specs; show her the business plan. Point out that you're committing a year of your life to this project.

Even though this has worked for a lot of people, and you can make a persuasive case, don't get discouraged if your first customer declines, or even if your first ten decline. I'm not saying it's an easy sell. You won't get every customer, but you only need ten. Ten out of maybe 200.

If you can't get ten customers out of 200 prospects to sign on at half price, then I think you've got to go back and reconsider whether there is a market for your product.

If you do get your ten, then you've got $300,000 and 100 percent ownership of your company. And you've got something else. Since you're guaranteeing their satisfaction and you're building it to suit these ten customers, you should also come away with a strong base of testimonials to begin your sales campaign. After all, your customer now has a vested interest in the success of your company.

9. Starting with Nothing

One day I came home from Carnegie Mellon University where I was teaching to find my son, Alan, lying on the couch, munching crackers and watching TV. I also noticed that he was looking somewhat dejected. He had recently earned his MBA and most days he could be found sending out resumes and talking to prospective employers. So seeing him home in the middle of the afternoon was a surprise.

I said, "Alan, what's wrong? What are you doing here in the middle of the afternoon lying on the couch watching TV?"

He said, "Dad, I've been everywhere and companies are just not hiring MBA people. So I don't know what to do."

"Alan," I said, "You know, you are one lucky son of a gun."

He looked at me puzzled. "What do you mean lucky?"

"I'll tell you what I mean. You could sign anything anyone puts in front of you, any IOUs, anything you want you could sign and what have you got to lose? I can't do that. If I want to take a risk and I put my name down I could lose a few dollars. I could lose more than a few dollars. You don't have anything. So in that sense you're lucky – you could sign your name to anything and who cares? What have you got to lose?"

He still appeared puzzled.

"Look," I said, "What I'm trying to say is if you can't find a company to work for, buy a company. There are little companies all over Pittsburgh where the owners want to retire, maybe they want to go to Florida, or they had a fight with their partner. But it's now for sale. Go find one of those companies and buy it.

"What's the worst that can happen? The worst is that the company goes belly up. What happens in that case? My guess is you lie on my couch, watch my TV, and eat my crackers, and that's what you're doing now. I'll bet you haven't even looked into buying a company."

He allowed as how he hadn't.

So the next day he got dressed up in his one and only suit, borrowed one of my ties, and went looking. And what do you know, he found a company right in Pittsburgh that was for sale. It sold paper goods to department stores and supermarkets and was owned by two older ladies who had inherited it from their father. However, they were not salespeople. They didn't know how to sell, and, as a consequence, they were not getting any new customers. The business was going downhill, but it had some assets. They had inventory and owned their building free and clear, and they were only asking $300,000.

So Alan thought about that and figured maybe he could go to the bank and get a $300,000 mortgage on the building and use that to buy the company.

At the time, there was a bank in Pittsburgh called Equibank. So he went to Equibank and talked to the loan officer who happened to be a woman. "I'm interested in buying a company," he said, "This company owns a building which I'd like to mortgage for $300,000 which would give me enough to buy the company. But let me warn you, the only thing I have in this world is the suit that I am wearing."

Of course I'm only speculating, but I assume that the loan officer was taken aback by Alan's honesty. "I'm not crazy about the suit," she said, "but I do like your tie."

"The fact is," Alan replied, "the tie belongs to my father."

So they went to look at the building and her assessment was that Equibank would be willing to give Alan a $300,000 mortgage on it.

Now he comes home quite happy with himself, and waiting for him in the mail is a job offer from a company in Boca Raton, Florida.

Alan asked me what he ought to do. His mother and I talked it over and largely at her urging, we advised him to take the job in Boca where he could get some real-world work experience. It wasn't my first choice, because I was thinking about going into business with him, but it made sense. "Alan," I said, "It makes sense. Go get some work experience and maybe later on we will buy a company."

He went to Florida and has done very well for himself, but I think the story illustrates a couple of useful points. One is that at one time or another, we all need a kick in the rear to get us going. Two, when you have the least to lose you also have the most to gain and very little risk. We can feel sorry for ourselves and moan about the fact that we don't have a dime in the world, but not having a dime can also be a blessing because it means that you can't lose a dime either.

10. Control

A lot of entrepreneurs go into business not so much for the money as for the opportunity to run their own show. That was my motivation, and it is the motivation for most of the entrepreneurs I know. Of course, when you are completely free to do your own thing, a lot of the things you do will be dumb. But they're your dumb things — not the dumb things of some smug supervisor.

Let me give you an example. In my first company, I told my partner I wanted to give everybody who came to work for us one percent of the stock of the company. That was my ideal for a business - all of us working for and invested in the same goal. It was a crazy idea, but remember, it was my first company.

Of course, my partner pointed out to me that we would run into a problem with employee 101, so we never did it. But we did a lot of other Roseman kind of things that were not so crazy and they wouldn't have been possible if I wasn't in control of the company.

Control usually doesn't become an issue until you go outside the family for money. And when you do, you will find that different types of investors have greater or lesser tolerance for letting you run your own show. After family, friends, savings and credit cards, most first-time entrepreneurs try to tap private investors, so-called "angels." These are high net worth individuals who may or may not require a hand in day-to-day operations. Typically, they require less control over operations than a venture capitalist, and that's what I wanted. I was already working for someone so there was no way I was going to start my own company and then have people telling me day-to-day what I was going to do.

It took some time to find somebody willing to give me majority stock ownership, but when I did, it was the best investor deal I ever struck. It was an angel deal. I was majority owner, and though I had to give away 40 percent of the company, my investor was happy to let me run the show. What I didn't realize at the time was this is not always the case.

Like a lot of entrepreneurs, I thought control meant majority voting rights; holding the most stock. In truth, stock ownership is really more of an economic issue than a determiner of who runs the company. Control of the company is really vested in something called a term sheet.

When you go for venture capital, the investors may want 20 to 30 percent of the company. The entrepreneur may take comfort in that, thinking, his investors don't have control. But any kind of professional investing arrangement will include a term sheet and the term sheet describes the stuff that the venture capitalist must sign off on before the entrepreneur can do it. For instance, the term sheet may say things like: you will not take or borrow money without our approval; you will not buy capital equipment without our approval; you will not give any officers a raise without our approval; you will not declare dividends without our approval; and so on.

Term sheets can have little tolerance for imaginative management techniques, and no appreciation for an entrepreneur's fun factor.

Of course, if I was the venture capitalist and I was handing over $2 million to somebody with an idea, I would want those provisos, too. But I'm not, though I have some very good friends who are. Rather, I am the entrepreneur, and the driving reason I'm taking the risk of starting a new business is that I don't want to be working for someone else. I want some freedom. I don't want to be second-guessed in my decision-making.

So, if control is important to you, be aware of the term sheet. If a venture capitalist takes only one point, but sticks in all those provisos, I would argue that from one point of view, that one percent controls you. My advice to any entrepreneur based on what I have learned for myself is that when someone says, "I want control," I would say, "Would you mind defining what you mean by control?"

11. Partners & Power

It's a cliche, but it's also accurate: A partnership is like a marriage, and there are good marriages and bad marriages.

I've had people give talks to my classes at Carnegie Mellon University who have had problems with their partners and say they'd never have a partner again. I've had three partners, and if I were starting a fourth company, I'd get a fourth.

Why? Partners should bring something additional to the business, something you can't bring.

Technology and companies today have become so complicated and so competitive that you almost need a team. I don't think a one-man band plays anymore.

To start a technical company and assume you're going to be the technologist, a hotshot salesman, and an expert at raising money and managing people is just not realistic.

Another reason to have a partner is to reality-check your thinking. For instance, it's my nature to jump the gun, to make decisions quickly. Fortunately, at all my companies I've had other partners who were very methodical. I remember one in particular who would have to look at a pen for three or four minutes, roll it around, take it apart and write with it, before he would agree that it was a pen. I would take one look and say, "Yep, that's a pen." They were always saying, "Roseman, wait a minute, hold on." And many times they were right.

Finally, sometimes you need to offload your concerns, and you need somebody who will listen and let you do that.

The CEO has to be the Rock of Gibraltar. He cannot go to his employees and say, "I'm not sure I can pay you this week." Well, to whom does he cry and complain?

But I would agree that no partner is better than the wrong partner. So how do you go about picking a partner? If you buy the reasons for having a partner that I've just outlined, then some of the qualities you want in a partner are pretty clear. You want somebody who brings complementary skills and thinking to the business. You want somebody whose opinion you respect enough so that when you have to offload your disappointment, he/she might be able to help you put things into perspective.

This next trait might seem trivial, but it's not. Ask yourself if this person would be fun to work with. Are you compatible day-to-day? Does he/she respect your judgment? Do you respect his/her judgment? Can you argue and still be friends? But most importantly (and I can't over-emphasize this) you want somebody with the same values. If four people are crooks, they'll get along a lot better than two people who are saints and two people who are crooks. On the other hand, if all the partners value integrity, ethics, that kind of stuff, they'll do just fine also.

If you decide to have partners and get this far, the next major obstacle you'll face is dividing the pie. It can be an emotionally touchy issue, even when the pie is more of a pie shell, so I want to give you a technique for handling it.

First of all, if you divide the pie equally, there's no problem. It's a non-issue.

But what if some partners are very senior, or some bring a lot of money, or others bring a lot of skills or credibility or contacts? How do you divide up the stock? Start by sitting down and mutually agreeing on the skill sets and other factors that will be required to make this company successful in a specified period, say three years at the most. You'll be listing things like technical capability, selling, raising money, contacts, administration, etc.

Make a list, then weight the factors. Do this together, and if you disagree, talk it through until you agree. That should be pretty non-emotional.

Now take your list of weighted success factors and rate each of you on your ability to bring them to the business. Rate them on the same 0 — 10 scale.

When you're finished, multiply these scores times the weighted factor and you'll have a mutually agreed upon measure of each person's relative importance to the success of the business. Hopefully you'll have done it without any black eyes or injured egos.

If you can't agree on what each of you is bringing to the business, you might want to reconsider whether you have the makings for a successful partnership.

12. Timing

I had some guys come to see me from Princeton recently and another one from Carnegie Mellon University. They were Ph.D.s who had a whole new way of securing data on computers. Their technology secured it both from outside hackers and from people inside the company who might want to steal it.

Right away I asked, "Who is out there trying to do the same thing?" They said, "No one, really — not what we're trying to do."

That raised several questions for me. Obviously these guys were smart, so I said, "Well, one of the things I look for if you're going to sell something to someone for cold hard cash is return on investment. If he pays $10, $100, $1,000, or $1 million for this product, at the end of the year, how will the company be measurably better off?"

I said to them, "If I've been in business for 20 years and haven't experienced people stealing, I don't get anything for buying your product. It seems to me what you're really selling is insurance. I think you might have a problem unless the premium is pretty cheap."

They proceeded to give me good arguments for why it's important to safeguard your internal data, and I said, "Fine, but you have to prove to me — more importantly to yourselves — that in this economy where people are trying to cut expenses everywhere, there is a market willing to pay to secure its data from people inside its own company. You think there is, but it really doesn't matter what you think. What does the world out there think? Given the current economy, I'm not sure they're eager for it. Maybe in a year or two they would be ready, but how much money will you go through before they're ready?"

Timing your venture is critically important.

You hear about "first-mover advantage." It means being first to market with something, and it's usually spoken of with reverence. Being a pioneer can also get you a lot of arrows in your back. One, you have to pay to educate the customer on what you're selling. Secondly, sales come more slowly because it takes a while to build up a sense of need. The sales you do get are likely to be to "early adopters," a small group of purchasers who always want to have the latest and greatest technology available.

As described in the book, <u>Crossing the Chasm</u>, by Geoffrey A. Moore, early adopters can give you a false sense of optimism about your prospects. Sales shoot up quickly and then you face a chasm where the bread and butter customers reside. Getting them on board requires time. I say, let some big company open the door, and you follow with a better product.

Young companies are usually on a short capital fuse. Suppose you go into business with $1.2 million in capital and your burn rate is $100,000 a month. If you are early in the market by one year, you've gone through $1.2 million and you're out of business.

In the 1960s, I came up with a great idea. Sell software. It was a paradigm shift. At that time, software was part of buying a mainframe computer. Some came with the machine and then you wrote your own custom applications. Either way, when the software malfunctioned, you knew someone was going to be around who could get it up and running again. That's why no one in the early '60s was interested in buying software. It just wasn't part of the mind-set of the times. If we had launched a business to sell software back then, in two or three years we would have starved and gone through millions.

Many years later, Microsoft came along and said, surely that's a business. By then, personal computers were becoming popular and the mindset about software was changing.

I am not the quintessential early adopter, but I was among the first on my block to get an answering machine for the telephone. You couldn't believe the guff I took from people who called me and had to listen to that machine. I can only assume the manufacturer was taking a lot of arrows. Today, of course, everybody has one.

Years ago, even giant Westinghouse had a policy of being first, second. What they meant was, let the little company open the door with innovation, prove there was a market, then they would buy them.

Assuming you agree with me that timing is important, how do you know if your timing is right without spending huge amounts of money on market research?

One red flag is a lack of competition. That tells me a lot. If you say there is no one doing what you want to do, no one solving that problem, the first thing I have to ask is whether it's a problem worth solving.

The other question is whether the customer recognizes it as a problem. Can you imagine going back in cave man society and opening up a store that sells sandals? You're an innovator, a pioneer and you can spout a long list of benefits for wearing sandals. But you've overlooked one thing. Unless the public perceives bare feet as a problem, they're not going to buy it. Your friends and neighbors may like walking barefoot.

13. Follow-up vs Pestering

The other day I called a young attorney I'm impressed with. While we're talking I heard him trying to stifle a yawn. It was 10 a.m., so I said to him, "What the hell are you yawning about? You're too young, and it ain't that late yet."

"Jack," he said, "I've been here since 2:30 a.m."

Now that's why I like him. He's got a job to do and so he gets to work at 2:30 in the morning to get it done. I call that "a sense of urgency," and it's an important trait for any entrepreneur.

The entrepreneurs I respect, the ones I really feel good about, are the ones that when they say they will get back to you tomorrow, they get back to you tonight. They have a need to get things done now because they know something else can come up in 10 minutes, and they might have to take care of that.

It also makes an impression on your customers. When you get a job, the faster you get it done the more it impresses people. If you think it's a two-day job, do it in 1 1/2 days. I've always been that way. If I can get something out of the way now, let me do it.

I don't think one company I'm familiar with is any closer to a product than it was a year ago. There are some good reasons. For one, they don't have the money to hire programmers. But I really believe I could have found programmers to do the work by now. Instead, things just go on and on, and I have to wonder, "When will they have a product? When will they have a contract?" It is easy to let time slip by. That's why you need a sense of urgency.

Now let's talk about persistence and follow-up.

There is an aspect of persistence that I want to stress. It may surprise you to know that some entrepreneurs are shy, sensitive and don't want to make pests of themselves. That's fine, but how do you know where the pest line is? How do you know when your efforts to reach somebody will be considered pesky and when they will be welcome?

For example, a company I was once helping pitched a venture capital firm for backing and got rejected. So they tweaked their business plan and sent it over again. It came back rejected. This exchange occurred four times before I started working with them. The first thing I did was look at their business plan, make some changes, and send it in unknowingly for a fifth time. I've written and read a lot of business plans, and I personally thought this one was pretty impressive. Three days later it came back with a note: "Forget it. No thanks."

I know it wasn't gone long enough for the venture capitalists to have even read it. I happened to know one of them and called him up.

"Off the record," I said. "Do you remember getting a proposal from these guys?"

"Yes," he says.

"Well, I really believe in this company, or I wouldn't be helping them. They have a solid value proposition."

"Jack," he says, "this time we didn't even give any thought to that."

"Why?" I asked.

"They submitted a proposal five or six times, and not once have they come in and worked with us on how to improve their business plan. They apparently think so little of us that they did not want us to work with them. Our concern was, once we invest in them they wouldn't listen to us either."

Now, I know my client. He's a sensitive guy who did not want to bother these people. That's a fact, but how do these people know that? So they took his sensitivity as the statement: "I don't care what you think; you can't help me." And then they reasoned, "If we can't help you now, we won't be able to help you when we put money into your venture either. You won't call us when you need help. It's a good thing we found that out now."

One of Pittsburgh's most successful entrepreneurs was invited to speak to an MBA class at Carnegie Mellon University when I was teaching there. At the beginning of his talk he held up a batch of letters and said, "I was here last year and I brought the letters that you guys and gals sent to me to apply for a job to work with me."

He paused and held up the thick bundle so everyone could see it.

"You know how many I responded to?" he asked.

Nobody raised a hand.

"Zero. And you know why?"

Another pause. "Not one person called me and said, 'Hey, I submitted a resume and I haven't heard. Would you mind telling me what you think and can we meet?'"

"Well," he went on, "if you don't have time to call me, I certainly don't have time to call you."

The moral? Push yourself over the pest-line. It's probably further out than you think.

14. Titles

Most entrepreneurs say they don't care about titles. I'm not sure that's true, but that's what they'll tell you. In fact, I don't think they feel any differently about titles than anybody else. Titles are important to people. Be careful when you hand them out. I didn't always realize this, but I learned.

I know when I hired my first employee at my first company, I didn't give it any thought. My partner and I were selling all day and programming at night, and we were falling behind. When I finally found a programmer willing to take a chance on our two-man company, the last thing on my mind was what would go beneath his name on his business card.

The day after we hired him, he came into my office.

(Now, you have to understand, it took a while to hire somebody, so we had fallen pretty far behind in our programming, and we had quit selling to catch up. Programming was the one thing on my mind.) So this employee pokes his head into my office and he says, "Excuse me, but I forgot to ask. What is my title?" In my mind I'm thinking, "Who the hell cares," but of course I didn't say that. Instead, I said, "I'll tell you what. I'm Chairman. You can be Assistant to the Chairman. Now just get programming because we're late on this job."

About a week later, this guy has business cards printed up with "Assistant to the Chairman" on them, and he's giving them out to everybody who comes in the office. So that's why I say be careful with titles. You may not think they mean much to you, but they mean something to the outside world and to the person to whom you give the title.

In all honesty, I remember the first time I had a card that said "Manager" on it. I was very proud of that. It's just human nature to take titles seriously. By the time I had grown and sold my first company, I had figured that out.

When another company bought us, the new management named me "Vice President." But my partner, who had just a handful fewer shares of stock than I did, didn't get the same title. So one day, when I was attending one of the management meetings for the vice presidents, I thought, "You know, this isn't fair. I'm here, and my partner is back at the ranch." So I announced to the assembled executives that I would like to have my partner given the title of vice president. Right away, one guy named Bernie says, "Jack, that's crazy."

"What's a title worth?" I said. "Bernie, let me do this. You can stay Vice President, except your business cards cannot say "Vice President". And any stationery you have, if it has 'Vice President' on it will have to be changed so that it has no title. And let's do that beginning today. Do you mind?"

"Well," he said, "Yes, I mind."

I said, "I'll tell you what. I'll give you $500 to take the 'Vice President' off your business card. Now is that okay?"

"No."

I said, "Well, I don't know what a title is worth, but you just proved it's worth at least $500."

By the time I became President of On-Line Systems, I understood the importance of titles well enough to maybe save the company a little money. So I tried an experiment.

I don't remember how many offices we had, but we were in cities all over the place and in most cities we had only one salesman. This was during a time when money was extremely important to the company. So I structured a compensation plan with this stipulation - you could take the title Manager or Salesman, but if you took the title Manager, your compensation would work out to be $1,000 less than if you took the title Salesman. I laid it right out and let everyone choose. The result didn't surprise me. They all took the title of manager, which ended up saving the company many thousands of dollars.

I think there were two things going on here. They wanted a manager title, but they also figured that if they became managers, they would eventually have people working under them and make more in the long run. So they'd take less now for future rewards.

And that's what happened.

15. Mission

Before you begin to do strategic planning, it is absolutely critical that your company has a mission statement. So what is a mission statement? A mission statement is a description of what service your company or your product is providing for the benefit of society. Don't tell me in your mission statement that you want to be nice to employees or that you want to make a reasonable profit or even that you want to maximize return on investment. Those are different issues. Tell me why you exist in this world.

Why is that important? Because I truly believe that if you are not doing some service for society, you'll not continue as a business for long. You may have some flash-in-the-pan success where you get in and get out, and that's that. But if you want to survive and grow and become the dominant player in your niche, you have to provide a useful service for society.

Now, you must understand how a mission statement differs from, say, a vision statement or a set of goals. Let me explain by an example. What is the mission of a fire department? If you are like most people, you will answer that it is to put out fires, but that's not really the mission of a fire department. The mission of a fire department is to minimize loss of life and limb and property due to fire.

Now some people become a little perturbed with me and say I'm just playing with words. I don't think so. I think that distinction is a big deal. The reason it is a big deal is because it dramatically shapes in a different way how you go about accomplishing your mission.

Think about it. If you say your mission is to put out fires, then whatever monies you get ought to be totally invested in better engines, better firefighting equipment, and more fire fighters. That's where all the money will go. You certainly wouldn't be thinking about fire prevention. That's not putting out fires.

But if you say the mission is to minimize loss, then you start asking better questions. Now you set out to create an organization that can best minimize loss. One way is obviously to get to a fire quickly. Another is to prevent the fire in the first place. So it isn't just a word game; it's a significant distinction that we make.

So I think you can begin to see that if you define your mission too narrowly or too specifically, you will never get where you truly want to go. That's why a mission statement is so important, and why it deserves serious consideration. It frames for you where you are going, who you are, what it is that you want to do, and why you even exist. And it has very practical implications.

Avis is a good example. Its president had the wisdom to raise the question of its mission. He had spent a long time trying to decide what Avis' mission should be. He could have come up with the mission that most of my students propose when I tell this story. He could have said the mission of Avis is to be a world-class renter of cars, but he came up with a different mission. He concluded that the mission of Avis was to be a major producer of quality used cars.

Now think about the changes that flowed from that way of looking at what they were about. For one, they took better care of their cars. No longer did they run them into the ground. No longer did they view the cars they were getting rid of as junk, on the way to the scrap heap. Now they took better care of them from day one. They washed them more and took them out of service sooner. The result of that shift in thinking was a huge jump in profits, because their rental customers now got a better product, the attitude of their employees toward their work was affected, and when they did decide to sell the cars, they got top dollar because the cars were in such good shape.

It sounds obvious or trivial, but carefully defining your mission can have a profound impact on your success or failure.

16. Strategic Planning

Remember that line from Alice in Wonderland? It goes something like, "If you don't know where you're going, every road will take you there." That was okay for Alice, and you may get away with it as a lifestyle, but don't try to sell it to a board of directors or to sophisticated investors. They'll want a strategic plan.

For an entrepreneur, nothing is as certain as uncertainty, and the most important tool available to deal with the discomfort that uncertainty creates is a strategic plan. All entrepreneurs plan to some degree, but a strategic plan is a little different. It attempts to identify and describe courses of action the entrepreneur should take in response to changing conditions in the marketplace.

What kind of changes? That's what makes strategic thinking a challenge — it means you have to anticipate events before they happen. Maybe one reason this is so hard is that it is frightening to think of some of the challenges the business might face. But it is absolutely essential, and I'll tell you why.

Business is a chess game. No matter what move you make today, your competitors are going to make counter moves, and you have to react. Not only that, but you could be blind-sided by new technology that will compete with yours head on. So now what are you going to do? And you have to move fast.

In a fast-growing business, the need for a strategic plan is even greater. One of the results of rapid growth is that there always seems to be a fire somewhere, and your first inclination is to put it out. The reality is that it's physically impossible to put them all out. And I can tell you for a fact that you won't be able to put out all the fires. You shouldn't even try. Some fires are best left to burn themselves out; they are just not that important. On the other hand, some may be company killers. A strategic plan should help you to quickly know which is which.

Strategic planning also gives you the big picture; it helps you see your strengths and weaknesses over the long term. Believe me, events in business strike fast. There is a tremendous pull to react immediately to every one. For instance, your competitor lowers his price to gain market share, and you have this knee jerk reaction to lower yours. Maybe that's the right move, but maybe not. If your product is feature rich or your emphasis is on technical support, then maybe you should counterattack with a service campaign.

A strategic plan also helps you decide where you want to take your business and which route to take to get there. It enables you to sit back and say, "Is this really where we want to go? Can we get there? And if so, how are we going to get there?" So, in this way, it forces the issue of positioning. In other words, it causes you to decide where you want to be five years from now and what you have to do this year to get there. Suppose you decide to increase business. A strategic plan can help you decide such basic issues as whether you should put the emphasis on getting new customers or on selling more to old customers.

A strategic plan is a model of the company, especially in its financial aspects. What are your sales going to be? What is your return on investment? What's your return on sales? Your return on equity? What things are you going to do to improve your current ratio and inventory turnover? Those kinds of things are used to measure a company, and when you have them you can do what-if scenarios. That's another essential tool, especially if you are considering growing the company.

There is one other reason for a strategic plan that is as important to a business as it is to individuals. It forces you to clarify where you want to go and who you want to be. Some people are comfortable not identifying those things. They say it is too restrictive. I don't agree. I know that in order to end up doing what I want to end up doing, then I better do certain things right now. And what I choose to do now is determined by working backward from my destination. A lot of people are confused about day-to-day decisions because they haven't clarified where they want to end up in the long run.

17. Ugly Babies

Entrepreneurs are uniquely opinionated. They have a vivid vision of the company they want to create and they are not usually shy about telling people why it's a great idea. They love talking about their "baby." That's fine. But entrepreneurs need to listen, too, and I have found that often the big ego that gives them the confidence to go out on their own gets in the way of listening to good criticism.

And it's essential for entrepreneurs to listen to their critics.

Let me give you an example. In my last company, I made a pitch to a venture capital firm. It was actually made by me and another fellow associated with my company, and at the end they were not interested. They didn't want to invest.

Over the years I've had so many people tell me that they did not want to invest in a company I was starting that, in all honesty, it does not bother me one iota. I don't know why. Maybe it's because I know that, on any given day, a lot of smart people will think the price of a stock like Microsoft is overpriced and sell, while a lot of people who are just as smart will see it as underpriced and buy.

That's what makes a market, so I don't take it personally. But I must tell you that when these critics were helpful enough to explain why they didn't want to invest, I always listened. Often those criticisms improved my business plan. That's what happened at this particular meeting with Fostin Capital.

The fellow who was with me didn't feel that way. He was not an experienced entrepreneur and got insulted and defensive with the venture capitalist. I thought that was grossly unfair.

Several weeks went by and I got a call from the venture capitalist. The guy says, "Hey, Jack, there's this company we're funding that we really like. Why don't you stop this foolishness with Actronics and be the CEO of this new company that we are funding?" So you see, it was good that I didn't take it personally because it wasn't personal. It wasn't Roseman that was turning them off; it was Roseman's idea.

Now I don't mean you have to buy into all the criticism you get. Consider the source, their experience and so forth. But you should listen. To do that, you have to get your ego out of the way. I know that isn't always easy, but it can and must be done.

It might help to remember that the object of the war you are trying to win is not to be right all the time; it is to create a successful company. Your goal is to understand as completely as possible what's actually going on. What are the facts? What is true and what is wishful thinking? That's why I am a big believer in market research. If my gut tells me one thing and the market research tells me something else, I'll go with the research every time.

I think that I have pretty good business instincts, but if I can't have market research, then I want as much feedback from the market and other quality sources as I can get. I want to hear a lot of qualified opinions. The most qualified, of course, are the opinions of the people to whom I'm trying to sell my widget. But professional investors can also provide valuable feedback. The importance of feedback is why the general rule in technology marketing is don't wait to get it perfect. Get it done fast, rough, and dirty; get it into the market and then let the market shape it.

Don't try to get it perfect in a vacuum.

And the worst thing you can do is give it to your engineers or technologists and ask them to make it perfect. They may well give you a razzle-dazzle product, but it will cost too much and its features may only be important to highly sophisticated technical people. Your engineers and technologists are not necessarily representative of the marketplace.

And neither is the entrepreneur.

Entrepreneurs are more like parents. They always tend to think their baby is beautiful.

But what happens when they enter it in a beauty contest? The advice I give to entrepreneurs is, if they really want an opinion on how beautiful their baby is, go to the top venture capitalists in the country who invest in their type of venture and ask them for money. Short of going to the marketplace, that's where you'll get the best judgments on just how beautiful your baby actually is.

18. Letting Go

One of the qualities of a successful entrepreneur is persistence. The ability to not give up on a good idea.

But what if you've latched onto a bad idea — an idea that isn't really a business opportunity? And you're thinking, "Roseman says keep plowing ahead, but it feels like I'm ramming my head into a brick wall."

If it feels that way, it's time to step back and reconsider. No amount of head-butting will make a bad idea successful. Now if your original idea is just changing, that's not bad. Most businesses bend toward the area that generates money. That's listening to the market.

But the question is: How far do you go before you say, "Screw it. This was a bad idea." Or maybe it's a good idea but not a business opportunity. The theory of relativity was a good idea, but I don't think a lot of people made money off of it. A bad idea is an especially hard thing for the person with the idea to see. The first time I bought stock was in the 1950s, and I was working at General Electric where we had this little investment club. Each month, three guys would pitch a stock they had researched. So this guy pitches us on Pan Am at $29 a share. He convinced us that it was a deal, so we bought Pan Am at $29. The next month, three other guys pitch their stocks, and when they're finished, somebody points out that Pan Am is now $15. So we reasoned if it was a deal at $29, it must be a steal at $15. There was no question, we bought more Pan Am. The third month comes along and now Pan Am is $10. Well, if it was a deal at $29 and a steal at $15, how can we pass it up at $10?

Well, maybe we were wrong at $29, but there is momentum to an idea and our idea was that we saw value in Pan Am that other people had missed. We were so impressed with our own insight, so carried along by the momentum of our cleverness, that being wrong didn't occur to us.

How do you know when to persevere and when to walk away?

The key is to look at your idea as dispassionately as possible. Sometimes that means talking it over with someone whose judgment you respect.

Not long ago, a young entrepreneur came to see me with a sad tale. For two years he'd been struggling with a business that still hadn't gotten any traction. Money had continuously been an issue, and he had just barely kept the doors open.

The reason he came to me was that someone he respected had expressed an interest in possibly buying his company and he wanted me to negotiate the sale. "Jack," he said, "tell me the truth. What do you think of my idea?"

One thing struck me as particularly unusual. Just that morning, he and a representative of the potential acquirer had gone on a sales call together and the prospect had invited them back. To me, that was a strong positive, but the young entrepreneur had been so badly beaten up by the previous two years that it was hard for him to stand back and take an objective look at his business.

So I said to him, "You know, I don't know anything about your business, but let me see if I heard you right. One, you just had a hell of a good sales call this morning. They didn't throw you out, in fact they said they wanted to meet with you again. Right?"

He agreed.

"Two, you have a high regard for the guy who owns the company that wants to buy you. I don't know this business, but he knows this business. And he wants to buy you."

He nodded.

"Well, if you have a high regard for him and he knows this business, then you must have something."

There was another indicator. In spite of himself, as he talked about his business, there was still an excitement in his voice that contradicted his actual words. It was clear to me, if not to him, that he had not really given up on the idea.

"There's a lot of smoke going on," I said, "no fire yet, but smoke. In other words, it doesn't seem to me it's the time to throw in the towel."

Each person's judgment on when to abandon his or her idea will be based on different things, but the determining criteria should come from the market, not your own wishful or pessimistic thinking. What is the market telling you? Does it value your idea? Do you see signs of it justifying your company's existence? The only way to tell is to examine your feedback dispassionately. Then ask yourself if you are still excited about the idea. It takes both a passionate entrepreneur and a receptive market to succeed. Walk away only when one or the other is missing.

19. Respect

When you are starting a company, an important measure to keep an eye on is burn rate - the rate at which you spend cash. Cash is always precious in the start-up phase and you want to stretch it as far as possible. Sometimes that means bartering. Sometimes it means doing without. There are lots of ways to cut your burn rate.

When I was starting my third company, Actronics, and we reached the point where we needed to move from our garages to commercial space, I sent the VP to talk to the people who owned a converted warehouse. They wanted $10 a square foot. We had no investors yet, and $10 was too rich for us. But I loved the space. So I told the VP to negotiate. See what he could get it down to.

He came back after a while and said, "Jack, it's $10 a square foot and there is no way they are going to settle for less." So we drove back to the warehouse and I went in and met with the owners, who were two brothers.

"You know I really love this space," I said, "but, I'm going to tell you right now we cannot afford it. If we have to, we'll continue to live out of our garages some more. I can't afford this space." One of the brothers said, "Well, wait a minute, Jack." And then he took me over and showed me the trim he'd hand cut out of hardwood and polished so you could see your reflection in it. "See all this beautiful board work and everything. I did this all myself. I did that. And I'm proud of the job I did."

"I think you should be," I said.

"Well then, I should be able to get my money, I should be able to get $10 a square foot." "Yes, you should," I said. "But you aren't getting it from me because I don't have it."

I went on to admire his workmanship and repeated how it was worth every penny he was asking, but explained again how we were just getting started and couldn't afford that rate.

"But," I said, "How about if during the first year as we're getting ourselves on our feet we pay you $7 a square foot. The next year we pay you $8, the year after that $9 and thereafter you get your $10 because that's what I think it's worth."

"Well," he said, "That seems fair to me." Then I added that we would need some warehouse storage space as well.

"How much do you want for space in your warehouse?"

"I was asking $7.50 a square foot," he said.

"You know, I can't pay you more for the warehouse space than we're paying for office space, so why don't I pay you $5 a square foot in year one, $6 in year two, and then we'll go to $7 or $7.50? When I have the money, you should get what the marketplace says its worth and I believe it is worth that."

"Jack," he said, "You've been so nice, I'm going to include the utilities for free. I'll pay for the electricity."

I said, "You've got a deal."

Then he said, "And in fact, I want you to do me a favor."

I said, "What is it?"

He said, "I want you to let me invest in the company."

I said, "You've got it."

The point I want you to take from this is that in a negotiation, if the other person is sincere, you don't get your best deal by beating down the value of what he or she is selling. Most owners are invested in some way in the property you are trying to lease or the service or product you want to buy. In this situation, it was clear that the investment was sweat and pride and workmanship. But even when it's not so personal, you rarely do well in negotiations when you demean what the other person has to offer.

20. Price Point

How much will people pay for something? About $2 less than they think it's worth. I say that because people don't buy on price, they buy value. And value is always less than something's perceived worth.

Take cars. When I go to buy a car, I try to bring it down to the lowest $10 I can get. It's a game with me, but most people do that. They negotiate. Very few people pay list price. What is it people do when they haggle over a car? Are they trying to get the lowest price? I don't think so. If they were just interested in price, saving money and getting the cheapest car, they wouldn't add all kinds of options back in. It's value.

I remember having dinner with the president of a large company when I was running my first venture, Heliodyne. In this case, the job I was going after had already been done by a competitor, but the resulting software was riddled with bugs and turned out to be unusable.

So I met this guy for dinner, and he explained what he wanted done. I forget now how much I quoted him, but it quickly became clear that even though the previous vendor had failed, their price had set his expectation of what the job was worth.

"You know," he said, "You're about double the price of what we had the job done for before."

I said, "Then why aren't you using them? Why aren't you using their software?"

And he said, "Because it doesn't work."

So I said, "OK, if mine doesn't work, I'll only charge you half as much." He laughed. "I'll even go further," I said. "You set the price, and I'll guarantee it won't work." We closed the deal at my price.

Another example of how your frame of reference affects your perception of value occurred when I met a research psychologist from American University. Typically, Heliodyne's jobs were large — in the neighborhood of $25,000 to $500,000. One day I met this professor and we got to talking about his research. He needed some help analyzing data, and when he found out I owned a computer company he asked what it would cost to do the job. I looked over the data and it was really a very small job. I said, "Small potatoes." He said, "OK. Then why don't you do it?"

We did the job, and I sent him a bill for $5,000. In software, at that time, $5,000 was truly small potatoes. But when the bill arrived he got very upset with me. "Do you understand that my budget is not big, and that $5,000 to me is a hell of a lot of money?" So I apologized for surprising him with the invoice and we patched things up.

Then he said, "Now, I've got this other job that needs to be done and let me show you the analysis that has to be done on this data."

"That's no big deal," I said, thinking how little money we were going to make. He said, "Well, what are you going to charge me?" So I'm thinking, we're not going to make peanuts on this thing, and that's the word that came to mind. "Peanuts," I said.

Warily, but wisely, he asked for at least a ballpark figure. When I told him, he flushed, clearly taken aback by my failure to appreciate the scale of his budget.

"Between your small potatoes and peanuts, I'm going to go broke," he said.

Price is relative. What might be small potatoes and peanuts to one person, isn't necessarily small potatoes and peanuts to someone else. And it works both ways. You can price your

Roseman

product lower than the other person had expected and lower his perception of its value.

That came up recently with a start-up software company I advise. The owner came to me and said: "Jack, I'm trying to mediate an argument between two of my sales guys. One says until we get some real top customers using our software, we should lower the price as low as we can go and get them in, and then later on charge our regular price. And the other guy says, 'No, we shouldn't do that, because people feel they're paying $10 for the product and then it's a hell of a job to go to them and say, now I want $20.' "

I'm with the guy who wants to sell it for $10. But I wouldn't say this is a $10 product. I would say we're having a sale this month or this quarter and I'm allowed to reduce the price for this period of time.

Books are written on managing the customer's perception of your product. But here are some key points to keep in mind.

When you set the price initially, set it with integrity, but remember it is common practice to discount a price early in a product's life cycle. We have all been offered pre-publication deals on books, pre-construction prices on houses and so forth. Early purchases help establish your credibility and fund the actual manufacturing. But pick your ultimate price carefully and create discount incentives thoughtfully. If you establish a reputation for rubber pricing, you will find yourself forever haggling with your customers like a car salesman.

21. Sales Forecasts

For the technologist or anyone else without a lot of management experience, sales can be a frustrating process.

While I don't pretend to be an expert salesman or even sales manager, I have sold and I have managed salespeople. For the manager or owner of a business, this is what sales come down to: hiring the right salespeople. Of course, that also requires facing the fact that you will make mistakes and have to let some of those people go. So the secret of sales — at least for the owner — is hiring productive salespeople and firing unproductive salespeople.

This may sound simplistic, but the nature of sales and salespeople makes this an error-prone aspect of management. The reason? A quality of salespeople is that they tend to be optimistic. You want salespeople to be optimistic. But optimistic people tend to see their prospects in a better light than might be realistic, so their sales forecasts are often bloated.

After a while, I figured this out. In the meantime the more I invested in them, the harder it was to face the fact that maybe I had hired the wrong person. My solution to this situation was to head off bloated forecasts at the time I hired the salesperson.

Now, in the initial interview, the prospective salesperson is going to tell me he or she is one hell of a salesperson, that he or she can sell ice to Eskimos. But how do I judge if this is true? How do I find out just how good this person really is? How confident? Resumes help, but only to a limited extent.

I would start by holding up my product. Let's say it was a pen.

Then I would say to the job candidate, "OK, how many of these can you sell in a year?" Now first, this salesperson will probably try to blow me some smoke and say something like, "Well, Jack, I can sell a million dollars worth of these pens.

Give me a job and you got it — $1 million in sales. No big deal. I mean, these are great pens you got here; it's an easy sale, no problem."

So I would then say, "OK, what if we do a little tryout, a six-month tryout? How many of these could you sell in six months?" Now the person will scratch his chin a little and look up at the ceiling and in a little more thoughtful way say, "Well, it'll take me a little while to learn the customers of this pen, but to get to a million a year? Maybe I could do around $300,000 in six months."

And I would say to them, "Good. But just how confident are you that you can sell $300,000 worth of pens in the first six months?"

"Very confident," he or she would almost always say.

And then I explained I was a very sensitive person and how I hated to fire people.   I would suggest this: "That $300,000 worth of pens sounds pretty good, and that's your number, not mine. So why don't we agree that if you don't sell $300,000 in pens, at the end of the six-month period, you just walk away. Somehow you'll just disappear into air. That way I won't have to fire you, and then I won't have to feel lousy. How's that?"

Now the job candidate would think about that and pretty quickly say something like, "Well Jack, yes, I think I can sell $300,000 worth of pens in the first six months, sure, but if you want to do it on that basis where I would just walk away, well, I think I'd have to go with a number like $200,000."

And I would say, "Fine. But remember, that's your number."

Now some people would look at me and say, "Roseman, you're a crazy man," because they had never been offered a job in that way. On the other hand, a lot of people took me seriously and resigned when they didn't hit their number.

But what was I really trying to accomplish? I was trying to get that optimism out of their forecast, get a realistic measure of what that person truly considered to be success and still be consistent with what I thought was a reasonable number. If he committed to it at the risk of voluntary self-termination, then I had to believe that he thought it was a realistic goal or at least he would work like hell to achieve it.

22. David vs Goliath

An issue all startups face is how to effectively compete with much larger companies. At my first company, Heliodyne, we confronted it after about a year in business. Heliodyne was a computer services firm in Washington D.C. We had been getting contracts in the range of $5,000 to $30,000, but our talented technical staff quickly completed these small jobs.

I was president and salesman. It took me about a year to figure out that going after small contracts kept me too busy to solicit the larger contracts that could take us to the next level. Larger contracts required a longer sales cycle, so going after them was risky. But, finally, I said to my partner Dominic Laiti, "Dom, I am not going after any more small contracts. None."

It was a bet-the-company strategy, but he agreed. We had enough small contracts to keep our people busy for just about a year. If, at the end of that year, we hadn't landed a major contract, we would have to shut down.

Almost a year to the day, I walked into the office and saw our entire staff huddled around Dom's desk, talking. This was unusual because they were usually at their workstations. I walked up to the group and Dom informed me that we had just completed all our in-house work. There was nothing more to do. It appeared that we had bet the company and lost.

Just then the telephone rang and our receptionist sullenly went over to answer. "Mr. Roseman," she said, "It's for you. It's NASA."

As it turned out, they needed someone to manage their national data center, which was a repository for research emerging from satellite exploration. The contract was for $4 million over four years. And the contractor had to employ 100 people. Heliodyne was being considered because our technical rating was the highest, but much larger companies were also in the running. I assumed one of them was IBM. At the time they were the biggest information technology firm in the country and already a big NASA contractor. We didn't have the contract yet, but I ordered champagne and we all moved into the conference room for an impromptu party.

The next day I was sitting around this table with seasoned government procurement people making a case for our little company vs. IBM. You might find my arguments for Heliodyne helpful.

One of them asked, "Given that you are a small company, how do you expect to staff this contract if you get it?"

I said, "I don't know who my competitors are, but let's assume one of them is IBM. Do you think IBM today has 100 people sitting on their hands just waiting for you to call them and say, 'OK, you have this contract?'"

"Let me guarantee you they do not. They will have to hire them. Now, do I have 100 people just waiting for you to say we have the contract? Let me guarantee you that I don't have any people available tomorrow either. The question you ought to be asking yourselves is, 'Which of us would have an easier time hiring the best people?' "

Technology workers understood and were attracted to stock options. I knew that a small company with a $4 million government contract would be attractive to them.

I said, "And if IBM screws up, do you think you could call the president of IBM at three in the morning? You'd never get his home phone number. On the other hand, let me give you my home phone number right now." And I pulled out a business card and wrote my home number on it. "Why do I do this? If IBM screws up on this one contract, is it any big deal for them with their thousands of contracts? You're just one of them."

"We don't have thousands of $4 million contracts. In fact, if we screw up a NASA contract, we might have to move out of Washington D.C."

I looked at them one by one, and I said, "Here is a commitment I will make to you. I will personally manage this project for NASA. I will be the project director."

During my year of marketing Heliodyne, they had come to know me, and they trusted me. I could see the wheels turning. Could we get a Jack Roseman from IBM to head this project? No. We would get someone way down in the organization.

As a small company, you work with what you have. IBM, Electronic Data Systems, Computer Sciences Corp., could all easily commit to this job and cite their track record with NASA, their thousands of employees, years and years of experience. Heliodyne was strong technically, so I built on that. I tried to turn our weakness into a strength. To do that, I pulled out all the stops. I think I might have even said I couldn't understand why they would even consider IBM when they could deal with us. It was guerrilla marketing. You come in and hammer away at your competitor's Achilles' heel.

Finally, we got around to fees and they wanted to give us five percent when I knew IBM was getting at least 10. So I said, "I'll tell you what. I guarantee you our fees will not be any more than IBM's." By the time we were done negotiating, we got the 10.

23. Tearjerker

This is about a man who could cry on cue, from one eye, his right one. Not that it matters. When you get a businessman to cry, one eye is plenty. It is unexpected and very stirring. Your gut reaction is to believe a man who backs up his point with tears, even if they only come from one eye.

Let's call him David. I was introduced to David by a relative when I was about to start a computer consulting company in Washington and couldn't find an investor who would put up capital without insisting on control. David had a West Coast company that did re-entry physics – mostly for the government. We hit it off right away, and he and I became buddies.

"Roseman," he used to say, "I see me in you. We are from the same pod. We think the same way. We do things the same. We can make music together."

So he proposed a unique deal. He would do re-entry physics on the West Coast, and I would open up my computer and IT consulting company in Washington. He had a novel approach to getting around the ownership issue. We would divide the profits according to who brought in the most business.

So we got this thing going and we were doing pretty well when one day I get a call in the Washington office from a guy who asks for David. I said, "He isn't in, but I expect him later in the week. Should I have him call?"

"No," he said, "Just tell him I'm not interested in heading up the Washington office."

I said, "I will be happy to tell him that." And I hung up.

So, after that phone call it was pretty clear that my buddy, David, was screwing me. I figured now that we had business coming in the door, profit sharing didn't look so good to him.

So, as you can imagine, I could hardly wait to get my hands around his neck.

Later that week he came into the office, as scheduled, and I said, "David, the guy you wanted to head up this office left a message. He's not interested in taking the job."

And then it happened. Just as I continued on with, "What are you doing to me?" tears started coming down his right cheek. He looked at me in this very sad and disappointed way and said, "Jack, you think I would screw you? I only wanted him to head up the re-entry physics part of the Washington office, not the whole office. That's you."

I felt terrible. I thought to myself, there I go, jumping to conclusions again. And so I apologized, we shook hands and everything was fine.

Now that evening, I had dinner with the CFO of the company who knew David long before I had ever met him. They went way back. As we were having dinner, I told this story, but when I got to the part where I was confronting David, our guest interrupted me.

He said, "I know what happened."

I knew he hadn't talked to David in the meantime. How would he know?

He repeated, "Jack, I know what happened."

I said, "OK, What happened?"

He said, "Tears came down David's right eye."

I asked, "How do you know that?"

And the CFO said, "Because when you catch this guy red-handed, I've seen it, he can't get tears to come to both his eyes, but he can get tears out of his right eye. And you caught him red-handed. That's how I know."

Now I'm livid again. I simmered on that overnight and the next day I met with David, and I said, "I think you were trying to screw me, and unless we come to an agreement that if I involuntarily leave the Washington office, you can't do business for the United States government for one year, I leave today."

"Jack," he said, "That can't be. All our business is for the government."

I said, "Why would I leave involuntarily?"

So we spent a good portion of the day arguing that point and I finally won. We got it down legally.

Later, a public company, KMS Industries, bought us. And David and I had another disagreement. So David went to the CEO and said, "I want to fire Roseman." This CEO didn't know me, but he said, "You want to fire somebody who works for you, be my guest. Go fire him."

"There's a problem," said David. "If I fire Roseman, we can't do any business in Washington, DC for a year, and KMS is doing a lot of work for the government."

He said, "You signed that agreement?"

David said, "Yes I did."

The CEO said, "I should fire you. Not only that, where were our guys when we did due diligence? That's a hell of a thing to buy a company and live with that clause. I ought to fire you." And then finally this CEO said, "Of course you can't fire Roseman."

I got this story from the KMS CFO, and it has a simple point. Here was a man I trusted implicitly. A man with whom I stayed whenever I was on the West Coast. I played with this man's children, joked around with his wife. We were one.

But were we? You really don't know some people until the

almighty buck becomes involved. It's a small percentage of people who are scoundrels, an even smaller number who can conjure up tears on cue. But you find them.

24. Problem Board Members

Selection and proper use of a board of directors is one of the first and most important issues facing an entrepreneur.

At many of the larger corporations, boards become rubber stamps for management.

This isn't good for those companies, but for a startup, a board without backbone can be fatal. You genuinely need smart advisors, savvy in your industry, who are willing to share their candid opinion and ask you hard questions.

Probably the most common mistake entrepreneurs make in picking board members is including executive-level employees and/or paid professional advisors. Neither one is a good idea.

For instance, I feel strongly that you should not have your lawyer on the board. You should not have your banker on the board. And you should not have your accountant on the board. Why?

Let's assume you're a startup company and you meet every other month. That means six times a year, on issues that will shape the company's success or failure, this person who works for you and is paid by you has a vote equal to yours. His or her livelihood hinges on the company's cash flow and stability. Not only is there a built-in conflict of interest, but all of a sudden this employee or contractor is put in the position of being equal to you when in fact, this person is not. It just doesn't make sense to me.

And there is another reason. How often do you think this person is going to differ with you in front of the other board members? Should they differ with you in front of the other board members? I don't think so.

Putting outside professional advisors on the board has its own problems. Let's take lawyers first. Entrepreneurs are risk takers.

Growing a business is full of risk. They say good lawyers never ask a question unless they already know the answer. Does that sound like somebody with a high tolerance for risk? Good lawyers have to be suspicious. Entrepreneurs should be suspicious too, but if they were as circumspect as lawyers, I doubt that many businesses would have ever gotten started.

Putting paid professionals on your board also cuts off competition for that whole professional area. If your lawyer is a board member, are you really going to have a discussion at the board level about which is the best law firm to represent your company? And that goes for accounting and banking as well. A lot of entrepreneurs feel that this is a way to save money and build a relationship with these people, but I say a board seat is too important a position for that.

Along those lines, be careful how many "money people" you put on your board. I don't have a problem having a venture capitalist on the board - and this will probably be a requirement for striking a deal with them. What makes this palatable is that you both know where the other is coming from. There are no hidden agendas. He or she is looking out for the people who put money into the business, and that's fine. But you don't want everybody looking out for that, as opposed to looking out for what's in the best interest of the company.

I've been on a board where everybody but me represented the financial interests, and that was a disaster. For example, if it's time to go out for a second round of financing, investors have a conflict. Suppose you can sell your stock for $10 or $20 a share. It's best for the company if you get the $20, but which one do you think this potential investor is going to vote for? The other danger with investors as board members is that most have never really run a company, and yet they really believe they know best how to do just that. They have helped run companies from the periphery, but sometimes it's very dangerous to know things from the periphery.

It is also important to have points of view other than your own represented. So you do not want to recruit a bunch of "yes" directors. You want people who have different views of life but understand what you are doing and sincerely want you to succeed.

25. Ideal Board Members

I want to recommend some types of people who will serve you well as directors. The first thing you should ask is, "What do I want my board to do? What function should it serve?"

The board can do a lot. It can help develop and hone the strategy of the company, act as a sounding board, recruit key people like the CEO and CFO, participate in financing ventures, open doors to the right companies, the right people. It can help in times of crisis, interface with customers, suppliers, the investment group, and evaluate new products, new businesses, new opportunities.

Now to be effective at these things, board members should have knowledge of your field and have operational experience. They should also be quick learners. They have to be smart as well as savvy. But above all, they must be people that you trust, people who you know are sincere.

And they have to be a little tough - independent. They should be the kinds of people who can ask difficult questions and formulate an alternative point of view — play the role of a devil's advocate.

They must carefully review and approve annual budgets and plans, not just rubber-stamp them. That's crucial. You want your board members to review financial matters very carefully because sometimes the financials are your best early warning system to serious problems.

For example, if revenues are lower than projected, you ought to dig into why that is true. A good board will ask tough questions. For instance, if revenues are as projected but the profits are off, a good board will ask why the profits aren't there.

At the same time, you need a board with which you can be completely open and honest. This is a very important point.

The CEO has to be the Rock of Gibraltar to the rest of the organization. He can't let people see that he's worried about how to make payroll next week. This means there is a lot of stress on the CEO. So if he can't cry on a shoulder, where does he go? I say he goes to the board. The board may be a very tough taskmaster but, in the final analysis, it is also sympathetic to the CEO and entrepreneur. So, when choosing your directors, make sure they're people to whom you would feel comfortable saying, "I'm in trouble and let me tell you why I'm in trouble."

Where does one find such a person? Network, and keep in mind that one valuable source will be former and current entrepreneurs. They are experienced, know what you are going through and bring a risk-taking mindset to the table.

To a large extent, ex-entrepreneurs are very generous with their time, knowledge and advice.

26. Ideal CEOs

A good CEO is a remarkable thing. He is a wily deal-maker, a tough negotiator, an enthusiastic leader. He is smart, yet knows when to trust his gut. She is also flexible enough to know when to get pride out of the way and make room for a good idea from somebody else. In fact, a good leader welcomes and values ideas from others.

This is not an exhaustive list. You want even more from a CEO, but the point I want to make is that good CEOs, who are willing to take on your startup, aren't growing on trees. When you find one who seems to have the right stuff, and that person is willing to take the reins of your company, it is easy to be intimidated on issues such as salary. Don't be. A CEO who demands a large salary or a long term contract is probably wrong for you and here's why.

I once interviewed someone for a CEO position at an early-stage company and this person wanted $250,000 plus a bonus. For a startup, that's a lot of money. But more importantly, it told me her emphasis was in the wrong place. What she should have been negotiating for was more equity. We were offering 5 to 10 percent, which is pretty standard for the CEO of a startup. At that rate, if she can take that company to $200 million in valuation in three years, she's now worth $10 to $20 million. And, if there's one person who has the authority and autonomy to get the company to that level, it's the CEO.

So if the CEO is good, and the company's technology is good, then why would a candidate quibble over salary? What's the difference if it's $100,000 or $300,000 if the CEO candidate actually believes she can take the company to where the entrepreneur thinks it can go? The CEO could work for nothing.

Now, the CEO candidate might say it's a marketplace issue, that he or she could take an equally promising technology to that level at another company and still pull down $250,000 a year while doing it. And, I would say "If another company is willing to pay you $250,000 a year and you believe in their technology, then you should go with that company. You should not come with me. You've got a better deal."

In reality, I don't expect a CEO to work for nothing, but I do need to feel confident that that CEO is buying into my vision for this company and not a fat paycheck. The formula I use for that is to ask how much money the job candidate needs to put food on the table. By that I mean to pay the bills, maintain his lifestyle, and if there is a spouse, to keep that spouse happy. But anything beyond that is just a trinket, compared to the wealth the CEO can create for himself by growing my company.

What a CEO candidate should be arguing is, "Don't give me 10 percent, give me 11 percent. Give me 12 percent, and I'll take no salary." If he wants the big paycheck, I can't help wondering if this person really believes in my vision and whether he has the confidence in himself to take my company to the next level.

Of course, there are many other things that can make a CEO wrong for your company. He could be all talk and no execution. He could lack a contact network. He could even lack a track record. But you can usually find these things out with some background checking. The thing that is harder to determine and yet most important is a commitment to your dream.

There is another reason for the CEO of a startup not to take a large salary. It's an operational reason. Taking a large salary sets a bad example.

At Actronics, my last company, I was the lowest paid person next to the secretary. That's a fact. I did that for a couple of reasons. When money was tight and someone said to me they wanted a raise, I could honestly say, "I make $24,000 a year. How much do you make?" And unless it was that secretary, they were already making more than me.

And when I was interviewing someone, and he said he wanted $100,000, I would tell him I made $24,000. That kept things in perspective. Maybe $24,000 was too low, but salary expectations start with the CEO. How much you pay him or her is important. You don't want people working for you exclusively for a salary. If you buy them with a big salary, how will you ever know what their real motivation is for being there?

Another way to judge a CEO candidate is whether he insists on an employment contract. I'm tough on that. If you're a CEO, you have to have a lot of confidence that you can get the job done. You worry me if you say, "I can get the job done, but give me a 10-year contract." If you're as good as you say you are, there ought to be people waiting in line to hire you if things don't work out with us. So why do you need a multiyear contract? And how does that look to the employees?

The fact is that most CEOs get a contract for six months to a year. Their argument is that it would take that long for them to find a job that they really might want, and I buy that.

Interviewing CEOs is also a great way to test the concept behind your business. If you talk to enough smart people, and they are willing to take cuts in pay to come with you, that's just one more confirmation that you're onto something.

27. Recognition

Poor execution is said to be a common reason companies fail.

What do we mean by execution? What can you do to ensure the best execution? The answer is hire the best people and motivate them by treating them like people and not plug-ins. That's one of the hardest jobs the CEO faces, but if it's done well it has a big payoff.

The CEO is also charged with managing communications, developing strategy, negotiating, planning, problem solving and many other tasks that fall under these larger categories. At least half of a CEO's time should go into keeping the team pumped up and engaged. I give it such a high priority because if you have the right people and they're committed to you and the enterprise, they'll make up for a lot of your mistakes.

Using material incentives creates in the CEO a false sense of having fulfilled his or her obligations to employees. Monetary incentives could reinforce an "us vs. them" frame of mind. Your goal should be to engage your employees in the enterprise as fully as possible. Give them ownership. Not just stock options, but day to day ownership. Make everybody feel they're in the same rowboat. If you spring a leak, it's everybody's problem.

Motivating people isn't complicated, but it isn't easy either. It requires relating to people sincerely, often when you would prefer to be left alone. Maybe an employee dropped the ball and cost you a contract, or a customer blasted you for a bad experience with one of your employees.

It doesn't matter. You can't hunker down, retreat or treat employees with icy indifference. You have to maintain a sincere relationship with your employees at all times if you want them to feel part of the company. It's harder than doing a cash flow analysis, but it's necessary.

Here's what employees want from you: recognition and respect.

At On-Line Systems, I used to walk around and say to employees, "If you were the president, give me one thing and only one thing you would change." Their answers always fell into one of three categories. Either it was a damn good idea, and I said, "Thank you, we're going to do that," and we did. Or, "That's not a good idea because of these other issues, which you would have no way of knowing about. So we're not going to do it." Or, "I have to think about that because I've never thought about it in that way," and I would always get back to them.

This effort can't be half way; it has to be for real - genuine and sincere. I found it did two things. First, it created a lot of good will just by asking for people's opinions. They were amazed that you wanted to know what they think. Secondly, when you ask employees to put themselves in the position of being the CEO, it surfaces a lot of their discontent, things that were eating away at them.

But I was always careful to limit them to one thought. That forced them to prioritize and bring out the most pressing issues. And once it was out in the sunlight, it tended to dissipate, but if they had kept it in their guts, it would have just caused more and more discontent.

The other benefit that comes from being open with your employees is that very often they can get you out of a jam. Yet when something negative happens, some CEOs try to hide it or spin it. Your employees are bright people; you are paying them $100,000 or $200,000 a year. You aren't going to keep it from them for long, and when they discover that you've been less than forthright, your credibility will take a big hit. In any relationship, the most potent cement you have is your credibility, and this is doubly true for a CEO. The people in your company must trust you.

Beyond that, these people have good ideas and a lot of creativity. Their skills are probably not limited to the narrow field for which you hired them. Tap that resource. It's not only a sign of respect, but it is acknowledgment that you are all in the same rowboat.

28. Decision-Making

Execution is a big subject. I read recently that when venture capitalists studied why their investments failed, they found it wasn't the technology and rarely were they wrong about the marketplace. The biggest reason their portfolio companies failed was because management failed to execute.

We discussed execution in Chapter 27, but I saved one of the most important aspects of it for it own chapter. The aspect of execution that I see a lot of entrepreneurs floundering with is decision-making. That's the skill I want to address here.

How do you make good decisions? The most important thing is to make them fast and make them with authority. Don't be indecisive. Putting them off is demoralizing to your employees, and it can be disastrous for the company.

I'm afraid business schools, with their emphasis on analysis and data, foster a tendency to drag out decision-making. I'm an advocate of market research and analysis, but too much analysis stifles you.

I know because it happened to me. When I had MBA people working for me and I would say, "Let me have your recommendation on such and such." At the end of that day they would come by and say, "We'd like to give you that report tomorrow." I would ask why they needed another day, and they would say that they needed to get more data. With more data, they said they would be a lot more comfortable with what they were recommending.

My answer to them was that every day gives you more data. Waiting for something like more data is like waiting for Godot. You'll never get an answer. In fact, here's a truism: There comes a time in decision-making when you have to decide.

Here's another truism: Every day will give you more data. It's okay to keep your options open as long as it's practical, but when it's time for a decision, make it.

Why do some people have trouble making decisions? It's simply because they're afraid of being wrong. It might help you to know that, in his classic book, <u>Up the Organization</u>, Robert Townsend claimed that if the CEO is right one out of three times, his average is pretty good. Sometimes it's the flip of a coin. The fact is, you're not going to be right all of the time. Understand that and go on.

I do not want to give you the idea that decisions are unimportant or their consequences immaterial to your career or the future of your company. I do think some people have a tendency to over-weigh the consequences of each individual decision, and that can be paralyzing. On the other hand, important decisions deserve the time and energy it takes to research the issues involved - to the extent you can get it quickly.

A lot of this is just common sense. Obviously, if you have a week to make a decision, then why should you rush to make the decision in a day? And if a decision is of sufficient importance, you find a way to get as much data as you can before events take the decision out of your hands. But sooner or later, there comes the time when the decision must be made. The worst thing a leader or manager can demonstrate to the people around him or her is that he or she can't make a decision. So sometimes even a wrong decision is better than no decision or a delayed decision.

29. Sweet Spot

More than 30 years ago I took a golf lesson. The instructor gave me a club, put this little ball on the ground and said, "Now let me see how far you can hit it." Once you have a club in your hand, this little ball on the ground in front of you and that kind of challenge, something happens inside of you. Something powerful.

I looked at that ball and brought that club back and down with all my energy, just as hard as I could. I was going to kill that ball. Well, I hit the ball. Barely. It didn't go very far. It just dribbled out in front of me.

The instructor said, "Jack, let me suggest something. Why don't you relax? Take it easy. You'll find that if you do, when you bring the club down through a full swing and the ball happens to be in the way, it'll go a mile."

I took 10 lessons in all, but I don't think I learned anything more important than that. I have applied it in my own companies and shared it with students I have mentored. I think there are times in the entrepreneurial experience when that simple advice is the most important lesson to remember.

Now don't get me wrong. I'm a hard-driving entrepreneur. I expect people to work 12 hours a day, six days a week. I didn't expect any less from me when I was in business. But there are times when you need to push, and there are also times when you can be pushing too hard to your own detriment, where you defeat your own purpose.

So, how do you know when to lay back? I would say when you find yourself flailing away and missing the ball. That's when it's time to take a deep breath, relax, step back and look over your fundamentals. Examine your concept. Make sure you have the right club to execute it, and then give it a full, relaxed swing.

The most important fundamental to examine is your focus. The would-be entrepreneur has got to know his or her focus: "What is it I want to be known for?" An issue I see in a lot of business plans is entrepreneurs who want to be everything to everybody. This is an age of specialization. You have to focus, focus, focus. The entrepreneur must ask: "What is it that this company is going to do better than any other?"

People, as individuals, have a right to exist. Companies have to earn that right everyday. What differentiator does your company have? What unfair advantage? Why should people call me when they could call a dozen others? What is it that I want to be known for? What is the position that I want to put my company in so when people think about X, they automatically think about my company? Those are the questions you answer with focus. You can't do that if you start doing all kinds of different things.

I mentored an entrepreneur who wanted to do two things. He wanted to do high-end IT consulting. In addition, he wanted to take a rent-a-body approach. I told him that all that would do was confuse the company and its customers.

Are you here or are you there? If I need five programmers, do I call you? Or, if I need a high-powered consultant to implement a half-million-dollar ERP system do I call you? If you say either one, you are saying nothing. To say either one is to confuse everybody. So I advised him, although I'm not sure he bought it, to stay with the high-end kinds of things and if he wanted to do the rent-a-body approach to create a separate company to do it.

When you feel like you are beginning to flail around and your stomach is tied in knots, it may be time to relax, take a deep breath and remember the ideal golf swing. Review your fundamentals. Among those fundamentals you need to keep in mind are the following: focus, differentiation, and unfair advantage in that order.

If you review these and you have clear and accurate answers to them, then you will find that executing – hitting the ball cleanly on the sweet spot – is a whole lot more likely.

30. Loyalty

There are times when what you stand for becomes apparent to those around you, and particularly, to yourself.

John and I were very close. We had worked together at a previous company, and our families even vacationed together. He was a brilliant computer scientist, but not especially interested in running the day-to-day operations of a new rapidly growing business. So he brought me on board as COO. He remained as chairman. John was not a natural risk taker, which I am, so in that respect, we were complementary.

After about a year or two at the helm of this company, I got a call from the CEO of the New York investment banking firm that had bankrolled us. He suggested my wife and I join him and his wife in New York that Saturday night for dinner and a show.

So we flew to New York and were taken by limousine to a fine restaurant. We chitchatted and, when we were done with dinner, walked out to the limousine that was waiting to take us to the show. That's when our host, William, said to me, "You know, Jack, I have a better idea. Why don't just the two girls go to the theater. I'd like to talk to you about some things. Let's take a cab to my apartment."

I said, "Fine."

When we got to his building, we got on the elevator and, when it opened, we stepped out into his apartment. It was extremely nice. It turned out he also had a house on Long Island, but he kept this for weekdays to avoid the commute. The item that immediately caught my eye was a backgammon table with a set made out of crystal, which was set up and ready to play.

On the way over, the talk had been ordinary business banter: what contracts were outstanding, which new ones were we likely to get, and so forth. But when we got into his apartment, he got right to the point. "Jack," he said. "We believe that if you were by yourself at the helm that would be better. John is a governor to the company's operation. He's holding up the works. What we would like to do is talk to him and make sure that he is set in terms of stock and a pension and everything else, but operationally, he would be set aside. You will have a commitment from me and the firm whereby you will take over as chairman and run the company as you see fit and we will back you. And you will be very happy with the compensation package we have in mind for you."

I would be lying if I said the offer wasn't enticing. It was the opportunity to run my own show and it was made to me in a setting designed to showcase some of the nicer things money could buy. I suspect it was an offer that my host was certain I couldn't refuse, but I did.

I was sure John would be well taken care of financially, but I wasn't at all sure he would recover from being squeezed out of his own company. Even more importantly, I couldn't betray a trust. Jack Roseman did not stick knives in the backs of his friends. I don't remember everything William said, but I do remember my answer.

"William," I said. "I want to assure you that the last day John is with the company will be my last day."

Well, he really got upset about that. He couldn't understand why. He was angry that I wouldn't go his route. He had put a proposal before me that he fully expected I couldn't say "no" to and not only had I said, "no," I said, "Don't you dare touch John."

Monday morning, John asked me when I came in to work, "How was the theater?" I mumbled something about it being fine, because I did not want to get into that discussion. But it's a story I often think about when the subject of ethics or integrity come up. It's the story I'm thinking of when I say that you really don't know what your values are until they have cost you something.

31. Attitude

Not too long ago I came out of a board meeting in which our strategy for raising money was debated. The company needed money. If it didn't get money, it would go belly up.

We had an interested investor and the question was valuation: Do we settle for anything the investor wants to give us, or do we try to play a little hardball? I thought we should play hardball, but no one would buy my argument. I guess I didn't express it too well. I was voted down.

Their argument was summed up in one board member's comment: "Roseman, do you understand that if we don't get money in here soon, this company will go belly up? We don't have any wherewithal to play hardball."

I understood their argument. When you're out of money, whatever people offer, you should say, "yes," because if you can't get anymore money and you say "no," you're going to be out of business.

That's true, but I was really upset at that last round of financing. The people didn't have faith that somehow, at the last moment, we'd find something. When you take that frame of mind into negotiations, you are demonstrating by your body language and by the way you talk that you are weak and can be taken advantage of. You can't do that. I never have.

I've been in that position, but I have always had the gumption to appear confident. I really felt that if someone called my bluff, somehow I'd get out of it. "If it's not you, I'll find somebody else," was my thinking. I think you have to go into negotiations with that frame of mind — confident and optimistic. It is necessary if you are going to compete, as long as you really believe that your position is reasonable.

I'll give you an example from sports. For every one time Babe Ruth hit a home run, he struck out three times. Ted Williams' batting average was about .400, which as you know, is a legendary average. Yet what it means is that three out of five times he didn't get a hit.

Now, even though, statistically and realistically, both of these athletes should have gone to the plate expecting to be out, do you really think that was their mindset? I don't. I think it was just the opposite. In spite of the odds, they expected base hits and home runs every time they went to the plate. People who knew them considered these men cocky. I say that was just their way of remaining confident when the data said they didn't have a right to.

The lesson for entrepreneurs is that, to a large degree, larger than you probably imagine, your expectations will determine the outcome.

In one negotiation, I wanted to add half a million to the price. My opponent said, "No." I said, "Well, you're killing a $10-million deal. Forget it."

So he gave me a lower price yet. I said, "Didn't you hear me? If you don't meet this price, there's no reason to continue."

He still came back low, and I'm ready to walk away. Then he said, "Jack, the only thing I can conclude is that you already have an offer at that price."

I said, "I do not want to have an auction or to tell you what someone else did or did not bid."

The fact is we had no one else bidding, but I didn't say we did. I said I just wouldn't tell him either way.

So we started at that level, and we negotiated up.

Does confidence assure a win? Not any more than it assures baseball players batting 1.000.

For example, a good friend of mine was negotiating with the government for a large contract. He said to the procurement people, "Unless you meet this price, forget it. I might as well leave."

And the procurement people said, "We're not meeting that price. We'll do this, but not that."

He said, "No, you have to do that." He was acting confident.

But the procurement people were, too.

"We're not paying that," they said.

So he slowly picks up his papers, slowly opens the door, and slowly walks downstairs. Just as he's ready to slowly go outside, he considers that no one is calling him back. So he runs back upstairs and says, "OK, I'll take your price."

That can happen. But that's not the anecdote I want you to take into negotiations. Think Ted Williams Think Babe Ruth. Think home run.

32. Worrier or Warrior

When I was CEO of On-Line Systems, a public company, one of the things I would say jokingly to my wife each morning on my way out the door was, "Well, it's time to put on my mask." What I meant was that I was leaving Jack Roseman the worrier at home and becoming Jack Roseman the warrior. I think a good chief executive officer has to do that.

There are different Jack Rosemans and, at heart, I am as sensitive as anybody. Maybe more. You might not believe that, but I am. However, I am not so sensitive when I have that mask on. When I have my mask on, I see the world as a stage where we're actors. And my role is warrior. So I take on the attributes of a warrior, a leader, a fierce defender of our company, our employees and our stockholders.

I used to smoke cigars. They were a prop that made me feel more confident. I used to smoke six to eight a day, even though I might not know where next month's payroll was coming from, when the next big sale was going to happen, or where I was going to get the next five programmers I needed to meet the specs in a government contract. I would be confident that the right things would happen. And they usually did.

When you are wearing a mask, it is also harder for things to get to you, the real you. You are a little tougher, not invincible, but a little tougher.

Now comes the complicated part. Good CEOs are not just tough, they're sensitive too. They listen and they worry. I would stay up sometimes in the evenings thinking about all the things that could go wrong, and become a warrior the next day to make sure they didn't happen.

That was part of my success in business, because I looked at my left flank, my right flank and my rear for what could bring me down and worked like hell to shore up that piece.

There were times when I got depressed. No question. When the price of our stock went down and I would get calls from people who owned as little as 100 shares, and who thought because of that they were my partners. They would ask, "Jack, how come the stock went down and your competitors' stocks went up today?" My standard answer was, "I had more sellers than buyers."

How do I know why? Did I enjoy it when we had some tough times and our stock went down? Of course not. That was tough and I was sensitive. It did hurt, but I couldn't let the people calling me know. That's why I wore a mask.

Being a warrior and letting things get to you don't mix. Now that doesn't mean I would lie. I do have a commitment to honesty, but on the other hand, I can't tell people I don't know where their payroll is coming from next month. But the truth is I am an outrageous optimist and I truly believe it will be there when I need it.

I want to emphasize for those people who are thinking of starting companies that you can expect a lot of grief, a lot of concerns, worries, depressions at times; headaches. I knew a top executive who went home everyday at noon to vomit. You need a mask.

You go through those times when it's tough and you have to talk to yourself. You do get depressed, but with a mask no one can see it. For instance, you realize you're not going to meet your earnings forecast. And you know nobody is going to remember last year when you exceeded forecasts. No, they'll just want to know why you fell short this year.

It was particularly hard to play the warrior after my heart attack. There were times I couldn't walk across the street. I'd have to walk half way, stop, catch my breath, and walk the rest of the way. I remember one meeting during which I went 100 percent blind. I could not see a thing. But no one at that meeting knew, I just continued on as if I could see.

That's a good example of that mask. My sight came back about a half-hour after the meeting. I am a pit bull. I always went on. I always had determination. My attitude is that if death will take me, then death will take me, but until then I am going to do what I set out to do. When you see things that way, you can take a lot more of the negatives in stride because no one thing is the end. You're on a journey in this world. I would argue that entrepreneurship gives you a perspective on that journey that nothing else does.

Some people say entrepreneurs are adrenaline junkies and they may be right. We like the highs, and that means we have to learn how to deal with the lows. That's just life. You can't have one without the other. You could stay in bed 24 hours a day, but what kind of life is that?

My son recently reminded me of something I used to tell him: When things are going great, don't be too happy because things will go lousy again. And when things are going lousy, don't be too sad because things will go great again. That's life and that's entrepreneurship, even if you sometimes need a mask to get through it.

33. Service

There was a time when BMW, Mercedes, Rolls Royce, Cadillac and maybe Lincoln filled the luxury car needs of the world. If somebody had told you that he or she was going after that market, you would have said that person was nuts. It was locked up.

Of course, since then, Lexus has entered the market and is doing just fine. How did that happen? How did those household brands lose market share to this newcomer? Let me tell you two stories, and I think you will be able to figure it out.

I drive a Lexus. Now, I'm driving along one day in my Lexus and I hit a bird. It splatters all over my windshield. It's a mess. So I come home and my wife, Judy, sees this mess on the windshield. Before I know what's happening she's out in the driveway cleaning it off – with steel wool. Needless to say, she got it off, and I no longer have a bird on my windshield. I've got scratches.

The next day I brought the car in for routine service at the local Lexus dealer. I explained how the windshield got scratched and asked if maybe they knew some way to get the scratches out. They said they'd see what they could do.

So they loaned me a Lexus to drive, and I came back the next morning to pick up my car.

The first thing I looked for were the scratches and they were completely gone. I couldn't believe it. So I called over to the service manager and I said, "Jeff, that's amazing. How did you get those scratches out?"

"We put a new windshield in," he said.

"What's that going to cost?" I asked.

He said, "Jack, forget about it. No charge."

Now before the Lexus, I had driven a BMW 733i. I loved that car and I took extremely good care of it. One day the clutch gave out, so I took it into the dealer and returned three or four days later. The shop manager said they had put a new clutch in the car but it still wouldn't go.

"You've got to give us another few days," he said.

A few days later I went back and the car still wasn't ready. I went back a third time and they had some guy from the BMW factory in Germany looking at it, and he couldn't find out what was wrong. They had it for close to a month. Finally, they put another clutch in and this time it worked.

So I asked what the bill came to and the shop manager says, $1,000.

I said, "To replace a clutch is $1,000?"

"Well, it's usually $300, but we had a problem with your car and therefore it's $1,000. It cost us more than $1,000, Jack, but we'll settle for $1,000."

I said, "My problem was a clutch that didn't work. And clutches cost $300. You're the one who couldn't get the problem solved and that's your problem. Why should I have to pay for your problem?"

He said, "Jack, it's $1,000."

I said, "I think you're being unfair."

But in the end, I paid it. I also never bought another car from that dealer. In fact, I never bought another BMW. He got his $1,000, but what did it cost him? I have a lot of stories like these. We all do.

Circuit City gave me free delivery because they didn't make a delivery on the day they had specified and that inconvenienced me. Home Depot paid to have a set of doors reinstalled in a new house I was building at the time because they had incorrectly positioned the doorknobs which resulted in the doors being installed incorrectly. They even told my wife to add some cost to the bill for aggravation. I immediately bought stock in both companies.

So what's my point? If you're going to operate a business, especially one that deals with consumers, factor in the cost of keeping them happy. You may have to charge a little more along the way to make up for that level of service. If you do, keep in mind that people do not buy on price alone. They buy value. If they think they are getting good value, they'll be a loyal customer. And now more than ever before, a high level of service is an important part of that value proposition.

34. Paradigms

In negotiations, your demeanor should be resolute but not inflexible, and you should be confident and relaxed. All of these things will be easier if you trust your instincts. Trusting your instincts adds an element of genuineness to your position and it fosters creativity. That does a lot of things. It adds unpredictability to your argument. Perhaps even more importantly, it enables you to change the paradigm by either being outrageous or using humor.

What do I mean by changing the paradigm? In negotiations, a paradigm is the set of assumptions shared by the people involved in the negotiation. If these assumptions are excessively weighted against you, you will want to change the paradigm. But since logic probably created the prevailing view of things, it's unlikely that you will be able to regain the upper hand with logic alone. You'll need a special kind of logic, the kind that is used in humor. Let me give you an example.

When negotiating with potential job candidates, some people would ask for an employment contract, and at that time, we didn't like to give them. So I'd say, "Do you know that my wife knows we're not getting divorced today. She does not know whether we are getting divorced tomorrow. So you want something I don't even give my own wife?"

They would look at me like, "Where the hell did this guy come from, Mars?" But it was effective because the argument had some obscure logic and therefore changed the paradigm.

Another example occurred when I was asked by the CEO of a company on whose board I served to help rescue a $1.3 million contract.

"The client has a new man on board, and he doesn't like us," explained the CEO. "Would you see if you can convince him to give us another year's contract? We can't do it, we've tried."

So, I went over there and from the minute I walked in the door, almost before I could sit down, the guy started screaming at me about how terrible our company was. They weren't getting good service. They were paying too much. Our people weren't any good.

I was sitting down now and he was standing. The more he railed the madder he seemed to get. Finally, he pulled up beside the chair I was in and jabbing his finger at me asked, "And why are you here?"

"I came here to ask you to give us another year's contract," I tried to say as matter-of-factly as possible.

"After what you just heard, if you were me, would you renew the contract?" he asked.

Now, I don't know what possessed me to do it, except to say "instinct," but I drew myself up and, in an intensity that matched his own, screamed, "Hell no, but I would hope you're a better man than me."

All of a sudden he started laughing, and then I knew I had him. My comment, which was not what you would call a persuasive argument, had changed the paradigm. Did I know it would make him laugh? The answer is, I didn't know. I just trusted my instincts. So, he agreed to give us another year and that's when I had another flash. I asked him for a two year contract. He threw me out of the office but, in the end, he did end up making the new deal for two years.

I said be resolute. You have to be. In negotiations you are staking out what's possible, and you have to establish these as concrete, tangible and firm. In one deal, I looked eyeball to eyeball with a venture firm and insisted on a particular point in the term sheet. I said without it there would be no deal, even though we desperately needed the money. They blinked, the deal was done, and the first question from my team, as the ink was drying, was what would I have done if they hadn't capitulated?

I reminded them that in negotiations, you always have the option of second thoughts and begging for forgiveness.

35. Santa Claus Syndrome

One year at On-line Systems, we got business we never
expected and profits were quite high. We were a public
company, and one thing you don't want as a public company
is a lot of fluctuation in your quarterly or annual earnings. It
confuses the analysts and your stock price can take a hit when
you don't show an increase quarter to quarter. Analysts like
growth to be in a straight line, preferably up at least a small
hill.

So, because the chairman and I didn't want this great year to
create unrealistic expectations among analysts, and because
we thought it would be fair to share the wealth with employees,
we decided to give out bonuses.

This was getting close to Christmas, and I thought I was going
to be Santa Claus.

The chairman and I went over the list of employees and, using
what I call the "infinite wisdom of management" criteria,
assigned dollar amounts to specific employees. It was informal.
We would look at a name and, based roughly on our perception
of the person's output, their contribution to the company and
so forth, we might say: "This woman gets $10,000, this guy
gets $8,000, and this one gets $4,000." We were just trying to
be fair in terms of what, in our judgment, they had done for the
company.

I have to admit, we felt pretty good about ourselves, pretty
generous. We had never given out bonuses before, so we
figured when these extra checks started falling out of the sky,
our employees would also be pleased.

What actually happened was they started talking to each other
about their respective amounts and if they got $10,000 they
were pretty happy. But if they got $8,000 or $5,000, they

were not so happy or grateful. So they came to see Roseman.

In my office they would say things like, "You gave me a bonus of $5,000. I worked, I think, harder than so and so, my output was more, and frankly I think that he could have done more sometimes, but that's his business. All I know is I did a helluva lot more last year and he got $10,000 and I got $5,000." And then sometimes they would confide to me things like, "To be honest, I always thought he was a brown-noser."

I thought I was going to be Santa Claus, and everybody was going to thank Santa Claus, but instead people got upset, they were among the few that got the $10,000. If somebody else got $5,000, well, that was OK, provided it wasn't them.

When the employees asked how we came up with this system, I would jokingly tell them that it was the "infinite wisdom of management" system. Some would smile, but most didn't think it was the funniest thing I ever said.

I'm a slow learner. We had started the precedent, so the next year, which by the way wasn't all that great, we had to give out bonuses, but they were less. So now the complaint was, "You know, last year I got an $8,000 bonus. I worked harder this year and this year you gave me $5,000. Why is that fair? I mean this year I worked more weekends, more nights and just generally put in more hours and I got less of a bonus. That's appreciation?" Well, I learned my lesson after that. The next year, bonuses were predetermined as a percent of profits and how much salary the person made.

That was the index of their worth to the company. We followed the formula and no one could accuse us of favoritism. They could argue with the formula, the algorithm, but nothing else.

So as Christmas approaches, I advise any entrepreneurs who may be considering handing out bonuses for the first time to consider my experience. Do it only if you can sustain the practice and do it according to a formula. Don't do it because you want to be seen as Santa Claus.

36. Motivation

Motivated employees are at the heart of any entrepreneurial organization. In a two-to-twelve person company, it is not hard for employees to feel a sense of ownership and see the impact they are having on the company's success. As a company grows, however, it's easy for the CEO to allow them to drift into experiencing their work as just a job, and that's something a growth company can't afford.

In the Executive Entrepreneurship Program at Carnegie Mellon University, we tell participants — and these are all owners of companies in the $1 million to $75 million range — that Fortune 500 companies can afford to have employees work 40-hour weeks. But in entrepreneurial companies, you must always try to have them working for you 24 hours a day.

So how do you get people to work for you 24 hours a day? There were times when I would wake up in the middle of the night and realize what we should have been doing at work. I wanted my associates to have the same experience.

So how do you maintain that kind of atmosphere? The easiest way I know is to ask people who now own companies to think about how it was when they used to work for somebody else. Did they ever have a job with good aspects? Then I ask them to identify what they liked about that job. They talk about having a lot of responsibility, being respected, being trusted, having their work reviewed, acknowledged, and appreciated. They talk about learning on the job, that their work was interesting, that it was a "fun" place to work.

So I say to them, "OK, now that you're the CEO, why don't you create that same kind of atmosphere for the people who work with you?" And that's usually a revelation because somehow we change when it's our company, we forget what we enjoyed when we worked for others.

A common mistake CEOs make is to think that money is the only or most important issue to an employee. When I was the President of On-Line Systems, I had a motto: "No one leaves this company for money. No one."

Obviously, on occasion, some people do. But I truly believe that 90 percent of the people who do leave a company do it for some other reason. It often appears to be money because if they're unhappy at the job for some other reason, then a 10 percent raise or 15 percent raise will be enough to entice them to jump ship. If they're really happy at the job, no one's going to hire your people away for 10 or 15 or even a 20 percent raise.

This is especially true in high technology where these guys are getting $50,000, $60,000, $80,000 a year or more. Why would they leave? For a 10 percent raise? I doubt it. If they leave, it is more likely because they were not being treated right. They leave because you are not motivating them.

Another mistake CEOs make is keeping someone who is borderline for a while longer. And a while longer. The fact of the matter is that you're doing no one a favor that way. Not only does that job not get done, but it distracts other people. It generates resentment and a lot of other negative emotions. It brings down morale.

A major issue in a company is: Do people enjoy working with the people around them? One of the first questions you should be asking when you hire people is, "Would this person be fun to work with?" Forget for the moment how capable the person is, because if he or she is not a fun person to be around, I don't care how capable he or she is, who needs it? In fact, another motto I used to have was: "If you're not happy working here, do me a favor and leave. I don't care how good you are."

I always wanted people to have fun. When you have fun, you're excited. When you're excited and you feel it's your company, you're going to work whatever hours it takes to get the job done, and you're going to have however much energy it takes to work those hours.

37. Self-worth

When I was 43, I was the president of On-Line Systems, a public company. I loved working, as I do now, but then I worked seven days a week, sometimes 18 hours a day. I was a workaholic. My whole raison d'etre was to grow that company as big as we could and make it as productive and efficient as possible.

We ran three shifts because customers used us 24 hours a day, and the customers who used us at night weren't any less important than the ones who used us during the day. But night shifts sometimes get lax. So I made a rule that when the phone rings, even if it is at 2 a.m., I want it answered within three rings. I told the night staff, "If I ever call and it doesn't get answered by three rings, I'll assume the building is burning." So of course I had to call.

I'd wake up at 2 a.m. and call. If no one answered within three rings, I would get dressed, go to work and ask, "Where's the fire?" That's the kind of hands-on management I was accustomed to. At that time I didn't give much thought to the level of stress it was creating in my life.

What I did know was that I was proud of On Line Systems and to me, its success was a measure of my own worth. The more I contributed to that success, the better I felt about myself. In truth, I liked being a hard-driving executive.

Then one Sunday morning in 1973, my wife Judy was surprised when it was almost noon and I hadn't gone into work. She asked if I felt alright, and I said I was a little tired, but that I would leave in another hour. She left to run some errands, and I sat there and soon began feeling like I was getting a sore throat. It wasn't much at first, but after a little while I felt short of breath. I asked my son to call his older sister who was playing next door and tell her I wasn't feeling too well. She came over and called the doctor, who instantly ordered her to call an ambulance.

In a nutshell, half my heart died that day, and the doctors told Judy they didn't expect me to make it through the night, but I did. Then I made it through the next night. Eventually, instead of thinking about dying, I started thinking about what life was going to be like with only half a heart.

I couldn't stand being idle, but there I was in the coronary unit at Passavant Hospital in the North Hills of Pittsburgh with wires all over me, commanded by my doctor to absolute bed rest. So I said to this cardiologist, "I need a recorder so I can dictate memos for my secretary." My doctor must have decided that I would be less stressed if I was dictating memos than just lying passively on my back so he got me a recorder.

I dictated more memos in the next two weeks than I had probably dictated in the previous year.

Another standard procedure in the early 1970s for a heart attack victim was to restrict visitors. They would only let your wife in to see you for 15 minutes at a time, two or three times a day. So Judy would be sitting around all day waiting to see me. Later, I asked her, "What was the toughest part of the heart attack for you?" She didn't hesitate. "You'll never guess. It was while waiting to see you each day. I knew the question you would ask me. And I knew there was no good answer." The question was: "What is the stock price doing?" She was right. I always asked it.

She said: "The doctors told me to make sure I didn't depress you, but I knew if I told you the stock was up, you would tell yourself you're not important, that it didn't matter whether you were at work or not, so that would depress you. And if I told you the stock was down, then that would depress you because you would feel you were letting the company down."

When I got back to work it was clear I could no longer get up at 2 a.m. and drive to the office to enforce my customer service policies. Nor could I put in the 18-hour days I had before. If I had any doubts they were dispelled when, for quite a while after I returned to work, Judy would show up every day at 5:30 and inform whomever I was with that it was time for her husband to leave. It could be a board meeting or a client meeting, she didn't really care. I always left, because I knew she was right.

I did begin to think that because I couldn't do as much as I had done before; I was less of a man. That was a harsh judgment, and it sent me down a difficult road. But I think it is also a common judgment made by men - and maybe women - who identify mostly with their work. At the time, I thought I was being realistic and tough-minded. Eventually I realized I was being simpleminded. That insight did not come quickly or easily, but it did come. Eventually.

One hint was the memos. For some reason, I saved them. When I stumbled across them, I was surprised how many there were. They made a stack about two inches thick. Out of curiosity, I sat down and read them. Now you have to realize that at the time, I thought they were important stuff - ideas that would grow the company. But when I looked at them later, you know what? They were about nothing. I went through all those memos and they didn't mean a hill of beans. In fact, I was embarrassed by the triteness of them.

My worth to On-Line Systems wasn't the number of hours I put in, but the quality of those hours. Because I had to, I learned how to get the same things done in less time.

Perhaps more importantly, I learned that we play in many arenas. Who you are to an organization is only a part of who you are. Who you are as a parent, a spouse, a citizen, a neighbor or a friend is also important. It's all these things together that determine who you are as a human being. That is the judgment that counts.

38. Making Acquisitions Work

When I was with On-Line Systems, we had an enviable track record in implementing a growth-by-acquisition strategy. We recognized that the future value of an acquisition depends on how the people at the acquired company are handled. Those people can also help to make or break a deal. That was certainly the case in one of our most successful acquisitions.

We were in the middle of our acquisition period when I learned that Atkins Computing, a U.K. company, was about to be sold to our biggest competitor. The parent company was Atkins Group, the largest engineering consulting group in the U.K. It was owned by Sir William Atkins, who wanted to generate funds to grow the parent. I got a meeting with them the next day and flew to London. They put me at the head of a long table. On one side sat Sir William's son-in-law, Philip Worthington. On the other side were three people who ran the computer subsidiary.

"How would you like to proceed?" asked Philip. "You know we have an agreement with someone. It's not formalized yet, but you are late in the game. Unless it's some unusual circumstances, it might be too late, but I'd be happy to show you the books."

I looked over at those three people who were lifelong employees of Atkins, and I imagined how I would feel if I had worked for Atkins for 20 years and then someone came in and looked at the numbers to decide whether he wanted to buy me, like I was so much cattle. My instincts told me there had to be a lot of resentment in these men.

So I said, "You know, Phillip, I don't want to look at any numbers. I want to spend the afternoon with these three gentlemen. I want to get to know the rest of the people in the company. If they, for whatever reason, don't want me to buy this company, then you could give me the best price of the century and I wouldn't buy it, because in the final analysis, it's these people and the people who work for them who we're talking about buying."

I did want that company. It was a perfect complement to On-Line, but I was sincere that I only wanted it if I could get the hearts and minds of its people intact. After negotiations dragged on for six months, and we had made an offer but heard nothing back, I got a call from one of the managing directors warning me that my offer wasn't high enough.

He advised me to meet directly with Sir William and talk him into taking my offer. I said I'd be on a plane the next day.

I said to him, "Sir William, I have been dealing with your people now for a few months and we're not getting anywhere. We've made an offer, but that offer can only be good for a certain amount of time because what I'm hearing is that people are getting nervous. If people leave, or if the people don't want to come with whatever company you decide you want to sell to, I'm not sure what we would even be buying. What I'm saying is that my offer assumes that the people I've met — that I'm very impressed with - will stay, and the customers will stay. If you take any more time or negotiate much longer with other people, I'm afraid we'll have to take our offer off the table."

"Will you take care of my people?" He asked.

I said, "Yes. I think that is important."

I got a call from their lawyers the next week. We concluded negotiations in an all-night bargaining session and On-Line bought Atkins Computing.

39. A Higher Authority

Books are written on effective negotiating, so I don't expect the handful of essays in this little book to equip you to go out and get the best price for your company. In fact, an important point I want to make is when you go looking for someone to help you in a negotiation - whether it's for venture capital or cashing out - finding somebody who has done it before is critically important. Experience is always valuable, but in negotiations it's vital.

Negotiations are full of subtle rules and personal techniques that people develop from practice. I've seen very tough businessmen lose in a negotiation because they pushed too hard or talked themselves into a corner. Because they talked themselves into a corner, they ended up blinking. A cardinal rule of negotiating is that the first one who blinks loses. That's why you always have to be willing to walk away. It's also why you have to mean what you say and be willing to stand by it, and you cannot blink.

When the person I'm negotiating with says to me over the phone, "You know, this looks like it's going to kill the deal," I have to say, "Well, okay, then it will kill the deal." And this happened. When I told this other person that it would have to kill the deal, he backtracked. Once you backtrack, you're dead. Because now it's obvious you're just bluffing, and I called your bluff.

So when you say something is going to kill the deal, you better mean it. And when I say it, I do mean it – at least most of the time.

An experienced negotiator can also assess how badly the other person wants the deal. I do this in a lot of ways, but one is by giving my adversary unannounced quizzes. I create difficulties throughout the negotiating process, little obstacle courses. If the other person gets hung up on these peripheral issues, then I know it's going to be a hard sell and this person will want it on his or her terms.

On the other hand, if this person is willing to go through the obstacle courses, then I'd make it tougher. It's a way to test sincerity and eagerness. The more eager somebody is to do the deal, the higher I would make the ante.

Maybe the most important single piece of advice I can offer is this: Anytime you are negotiating for something, whether it's selling your company or terms of a venture investment, have other people waiting in line.

I don't know how many times I've heard entrepreneurs say, "We have to take this deal because there are no other companies prepared to buy this company, even for the ballpark of this price." Or, "We have to take this venture capital deal, because there's no one else in line." Once you take on that mentality, you may very well be the loser.

Even if people aren't waiting in line to buy your company or invest in it, what you want to do is create an aura that there are.

One time I was selling a company and I said, "You know, if you're not prepared to pay 'X' million, then I don't think we should go on."

And the prospective buyer said, "Is that because you've already gotten an offer for 'X' million?"

I said, "I can't answer that. I don't think it would be fair to whoever may be in line. So I will not tell you that there is. I won't tell you that there isn't."

That created an aura that there were other buyers, but I didn't say that. I didn't lie. I said, "I can't tell you." It's best if you actually do have people waiting in line, but it's not essential.

40. Outrageous Optimism

It takes a lot of optimism to start a new company. It takes more than optimism. When you consider the odds, the barriers and the almost daily obstacles to success, it takes outrageous optimism. Outrageous optimism is more optimism than your average, reasonably bright person has any right to possess. So how do some people come to have such a bright outlook? Where does it come from? An entrepreneurial father? If so, I am a very unlikely candidate.

I grew up in poverty in Lynn, Massachusetts, in one of the poorest ethnic ghettos within that city. Among our neighbors, I did not know of anyone who was less well off than we were. Our apartment was so small my brother and I shared the same bed through high school and the only place I could find the quiet to do my homework was in the john (which made me very unpopular).

It so happened that my father was an entrepreneur — a skilled tailor. But he had a problem with price point. In Germany he had gotten $14 a week, but the going rate in America was $12. Unwilling to bend on this assessment of his value, he didn't work most of the time.

When he did find work, it was during Easter and Christmas when the workload was such that they just needed him and paid his $14. This taught me a lot about sticking to my principles, but certainly not that good things flow from an optimistic attitude.

A mentor? A neighborhood entrepreneur? Entrepreneurs in our neighborhood were always being broken into, so I did not admire them. And my friends were as often as not doing the breaking-in. I saw no long-term future in their idea of entrepreneurship.

An entrepreneurial mother? I lost one of my brothers and his whole family in Nazi concentration camps before we could afford to bring what was left of our family to the U.S. It seemed to me that my mother's sadness or guilt over that was forever in the background of our lives. It's hard to remember times when she wasn't crying, which does not foster a bright outlook in your children.

The one exception I recall was when she went shopping. She would always look at the price tag and immediately summon the owner. "This price," she would say, "is for rich people. We are not rich people. How much is it for us?" And the owner would be amused by this and give her a break.

My adversaries? What sometimes gets lost in the horror of the Holocaust, is that life for Jews in America at that time was not as easy as some people think. Anti-Semitism was widespread. Older kids in school would catch me between floors and ask if I was a Jew and then punch me.

One time I asked if it mattered if one of my parents was a Jew and the other one wasn't. (It didn't). Another time I had a gang of boys put out a cigarette in my hand. Does any of this build optimism? I don't really know.

When I try to tell my own children how it was in those days, they say, "We know, Dad, you had to walk barefoot two miles to school in a foot of snow, and it was uphill both ways."

The truth is I don't know where my optimism comes from, but it's true that I am naturally positive. It may be harder for others to be positive, I don't know. The only time I had doubts was after my heart attack, and eventually, I worked through them. What I do know is that I've seen expectations shape experience far too often to doubt that optimism is a keystone in entrepreneurial and other success. Another way of saying the same thing is that success breeds success. On the other hand, I've seen failure grind people down so far they were never able to shake their self-doubts.

Entrepreneurs can't afford to let that happen. Inevitably you will fail now and then, generally on a scale comparable to your dream. You don't go down easily. You don't go quickly and you don't go down without a fight. If you have to go down, then just learn what you can from it and move on.

They say an optimist sees a glass of water half full instead of half empty. An entrepreneur looks at that same glass of water and because he or she is an outrageous optimist, sees a crystal goblet of wine.

Without that kind of confidence, entrepreneurs would not have the underlying hopefulness to leave what they know behind and set off into new and unknown territory, inventing the road as they go.

So if you ask me where outrageous optimism comes from, my best guess is it's the confidence that you have within you, the imagination and determination to fulfill a need in the marketplace. You may not know exactly how the glass becomes crystal or the water wine, but you somehow know you will bring everything you are to bear on getting the job done.

41. Wake-Up Call

As I've described earlier, in 1973 I had a major heart attack that left me with half my heart clinically dead. The doctors told my wife I might not live through the night. For a while, any time I felt a little pain in my chest I would think, "Okay God, here I come."

Heart damage is very difficult to get used to. The doctors advise anytime you have chest pains to spray or place a pill of nitroglycerin under your tongue. If you still have pain fifteen minutes later, do it again. If that doesn't work, and you are still alive, go to an emergency room. But if you go to an emergency room with my history and say you have chest pain, you better have a couple of days coming up with nothing to do because you're in for at least 24 hours, maybe 48. Whereas, if you just lay down, in three hours you might feel perfect again. But at my age, with my history, once you go to an emergency room, they won't let you out. That's happened to me so many times I am very reluctant to go to an emergency room again.

As a result, I have had to learn to deal with this periodic reminder that any day could be my last. So I turned it around. Until a student gave me the watch I am wearing, I used to have one that had an alarm on it. I set it so that every night at midnight the alarm would ring and that would remind me that I had lived another day. That trained me not to take any day for granted. Since I don't wear that watch anymore, I now have the alarm set in my home office where at midnight it still rings.

In 1982, I went in for quadruple bypass surgery and since then three of the four vessels have closed.

Now the issue is, half the heart is good, half is dead, three of the four vessels are closed. How many more years do I have? All I can tell you is that at the age of 50 we had quite a party

Roseman   151 because I never thought I would make 50. At 60, we had a bigger party because I certainly never thought I would be 60. And not too long ago we had a 10-day blast because I made 70.

I explain this to you, not to rub in the fact that you missed three great parties, but because living this way has taught me many lessons.

One is that I may not be around tomorrow. I take that as a given, so it makes each day a little more special. You may not be around tomorrow, either, but I doubt you think about it much. The truth is, no one is guaranteeing you tomorrow. God forbid, but you could walk across the street and get run over by a truck. And the fact is that several friends younger than I am, many of whom I've played gin with regularly over the years, have died and I'm still alive. Go figure.

So that is one point. Don't take any day for granted. In that sense I've been blessed because I don't take any day for granted.

The second point is that even though I'm not religious in the conventional sense, I view myself as spiritual. I have to believe that there has been a reason that I've lived these 30 years since my original heart attack. That fact has given a sense of mission and purpose to my life that was not as clear before I had my heart attack, and that mission is to give back, to make society just a tiny bit better. I think we all need a mission and each of us needs a purpose in life. After my heart attack, three doctors told me I would never work again. Well, I'm still working, because I have a mission.

The third lesson is that since we don't know who's number is up tomorrow, we should live as best and as much as we can so that on the day we die we have the fewest 'should haves and could haves'. And each person has to decide exactly what that means for them.

I can tell you for a fact, if this were my last day I would have no 'could haves or should haves'. That's the way I've lived these 30 years.

People do not have to go through a heart attack to appreciate each day. At least they should not have to.

This ties into an experience I had on the Carnegie Mellon University Campus where I heard a student sigh and say, "Good thing today is Friday because now I've got two days to live." That meant this young fellow in his 20s was enjoying two days out of seven and dreading the other five. How many people think that's the way life has to be?

I was eating a chocolate ice cream cone the other day and it got me thinking. Before I knew it, I had gobbled down 95 percent of that cone and there was just a little bit left. I love chocolate ice cream. I loved that cone, and I thought, "How do I make that flavor last as long as I can." So I took a smaller lick, really tasted the chocolate in my mouth, and then took another little lick. I tried to postpone finishing it as long as possible.

It seems to me that is what happens in life. We rush through the best of it thoughtlessly, and it's only when we can see the end in sight do we begin to slow down enough to appreciate how precious each day really is. I got a wake-up call early enough in my life to enrich immeasurably these last 30 years, though I don't necessarily recommend my method to anyone else. Hopefully just thinking about that ice cream cone will slow you down enough so you don't miss what's really important.